The Cuckoo on the Kettle

━ *The* ━
CUCKOO
on the
KETTLE

Joan Grant

with a Foreword by
Bill Oddie

WHITTET BOOKS

First published 1993

© 1993 by Joan Grant
Illustrations © 1993 by John Cox

Whittet Books Ltd, 18 Anley Road, London W14 0BY

The right of Joan Grant to be identified as
the author of this work has been
asserted in accordance with the Copyright,
Designs and Patents Act 1988

Design by Paul Minns

British Library Cataloguing in Publication Data
A catalogue record for this book
is available from the British Library

ISBN 1 873580 05 3

Typeset by Litho Link Ltd, Welshpool, Powys, Wales
Printed and bound by Bath Press

Contents

'From troubles of the world
I turn to ducks . . .'
            F.W. Harvey

Foreword

I am a birdwatcher. I am also a bird lover. Are they one and the same? I'm beginning to wonder. These days bird watching has got awfully technical. More and more people seem totally obsessed with chasing rarities (often called 'twitching'). Nothing wrong with that. It's undeniably exciting to see a rare bird, but it does seem to me to reduce the whole thing to the level of ornithological train spotting. Mind you, there's nothing wrong with train spotting either. But surely the real train enthusiasts stop and admire the engines now and then? They don't just think of them as numbers in a book. In the same way, I hope most twitchers don't just think of the birds as names to be ticked off on a check list. But, like I said, I'm beginning to wonder. Let me tell you a little story . . .

A few years ago a very rare tern was spotted at a Midlands reservoir. Birdwatchers travelled from all over the country to see it. It soon became obvious that the bird was not in a very healthy condition (perhaps not surprising since it had been blown thousands of miles off course away from its normally tropical habitat and natural food supply). Some of the birdwatchers became concerned enough to suggest catching the bird so it could be cared for or even put on a plane back home. However, amazingly, not everyone was happy with this idea. Twitchers all over Britain had got news of the bird on 'Birdline' and were keeping in touch by mobile phone or CB radio (I told you things have got very technical!). When they heard that there were plans to 'rescue' the tern some of them were horrified. The thing is, once a bird is in a cardboard-box or a cage it has become 'captive' and you can't tick it. The bird's condition visibly deteriorated as the argument continued: should it be captured or left for more people to add it to their lists? Finally, nature administered an ironic justice. As the next dawn broke, phalanxes of binoculars scanned the reservoir. The rare tern was nowhere to be seen. Until someone spotted it floating by a shingle bank. Dead. You can't tick a dead bird either.

Now, of course, I'm not saying that all birdwatchers or twitchers are heartless. There is a widely publicized – and adhered to – code of conduct, and rule number one is: 'the welfare of the bird MUST come first'. But still I often wonder how many of them really CARE?

How many would rather tick a sick rarity than miss a healthy one? How many take as much pleasure in the beauty and character of common birds? How many would regard the idea of a bird hospital as purely sentimental? How many would 'bother' to read this book?

Joan Grant probably wouldn't call herself a birdwatcher. But bird lover she surely is, and on a remarkable scale: huge heart, tiny premises. (Read on and you'll find out what I mean.) She always gives her patients human names. She also talks to them. Call it sentimental if you like, but it is more truly an indication of what the birds mean to her and indeed what clearly she means to them.

Quite simply, Joan Grant gives LIFE to birds. I dare say she would agree that the birds give LIFE to her. This book is full of it. I defy the most hardened twitcher to read it and remain uncharmed or unmoved!

You'll love it!

BILL ODDIE

1

On the Move

We moved on a Good Friday: lock, stock and wild bird hospital. While cars were belting along the main road heading for all points west in the mad, Easter rush, my husband, Eric, and I were carting our worldly goods to a funny little prefab place known as 'the Chalet'. Originally it had been a small summer house and was hidden behind some trees and bushes in the grounds of the old house we'd been living in as tenants; we'd occupied two small rooms on the ground floor. So we didn't have far to go. It had been added to over the years and as well as the small bedroom and sitting-room it now boasted a little kitchen and a tiny bathroom, the latter measuring six foot by five.

'It'll never go through that doorway,' grunted Eric, wrestling with a hefty chest-of-drawers. The Chalet was partly furnished but we were bringing some of the old furniture over from our vacated rooms.

'Yes, it will, it's *got* to,' I said emphatically. 'Push!'

There was a scraping noise and a sliver of wood fell off. '*Push!*' I yelled again.

'I am doing,' yelled back Eric. 'Lift your end a bit . . . that's right. Higher!'

'I can't move . . . lift yours,' I groaned, struggling to support a dark mountain of solid oak.

Somehow we got it through the first door – our new abode had only one entrance – but then the old chest-of-drawers had to be manipulated through a second narrow doorway at immediate right-angles to the other.

At last we got it into the sitting-room and into position. That was *my* chest-of-drawers. Now there was another large one – Eric's. No room in the bedroom for either; they'd have to go side by side against the sitting-room wall. We had another struggle . . .

'We've got too much rubbish, that's the trouble,' grumbled Eric minutes later as he staggered down the gravel path dropping things right, left and centre. 'Half of this wants chucking out.' Returning to the two rooms we were leaving for this desirable residence he grabbed hold of a large box.

'Don't touch that . . . that's Lucy!' I cried, my arms full of bedclothes. Lucy was my little invalid mallard duck with a twisted, crippled leg. She was waiting to be moved along with the other birds.

'I'm moving the birds last of all,' I explained. 'When things are sorted out.'

'Sorted out? You must be joking!' snorted Eric. 'I shouldn't think we'll ever be sorted out.'

'I'll make a nice cup of tea in a minute,' I said soothingly, hunting for a kettle. There wasn't one; an electric kettle went on the growing list of things to buy. I filled a saucepan with water . . .

Somehow we manipulated our two beds and various chairs and bits and pieces through the awkward doorways, but only with great difficulty and much swearing.

'We'll never get all this stuff in,' said Eric gloomily, prodding a tea-bag in a large mug. 'There's all those ruddy cages yet.'

'I know.' I sighed, suddenly feeling very weary. All those ruddy cages contained Wol, my tawny owl; Katy, a fairly new arrival – a kestrel; Bully, an elderly bullfinch; Chloe, a greenfinch; Lucy, the duck; Crusoe, my old crow; and various other newish patients not yet named, including two blackbirds, a sparrow and a very niggly moorhen. I wasn't at all sure where they were all going. Although, in theory, there was more actual floor space in our new home, the ceilings were low and I could no longer stack the cages as I had done before in my little bedsit. Nor was there the large wardrobe that had been in Eric's old room on which I used to stack boxes and even a sack of hay; in his new little square bedroom there was only a fitted cupboard. There were no outhouses or aviaries; all the birds had to be accommodated indoors.

I had also acquired two very large and strongly made cardboard-boxes which I needed for the birds; where on earth would *they* go? There were going to be problems . . .

By the end of the day, however, we had two beds to sleep in and things were looking a bit more orderly. I'd spent a good deal of time grovelling on the floor sweeping up dead woodlice from under the damp newspaper that apparently served as felt underneath the carpet in the corner where my bed would be. Well, I supposed they were better than live ones.

Crusoe, my rather crotchety invalid crow, was installed in his large cardboard cage on top of one of the chest-of-drawers. The Twilweld wire door of the cage dropped downwards and was open – he hated it closed – and he'd been perched on the edge, leaning out and very interested in all that had been going on. Across from my bed the two little finches were in 'Clara's Cage' on a long, low table; it had been called Clara's Cage ever since it was made, years ago, for a little collared dove of that name. Over this I heaved Katy in her much larger cage: the kestrel had two broken wings and hadn't been with me very long; Pam, my friend with the bird hospital some miles away, had brought her over; she'd had Katy three years, she told me. Wol, my intrepid owl, was in the other large wooden cage on top of one of the new boxes at the foot of my bed. He was five years old and I'd had him since he was a small fledgling. Facing across the room, his head bobbed madly as he surveyed the strange new scene. Wol wasn't at all sure he liked what he saw. On top of these last two cages I heaved a long and large cardboard cage I'd had for some time.

Lucy was in her box on my old trunk at the foot of Eric's bed. He didn't mind Lucy the duck as a room-mate; she was quiet at night and didn't disturb him, he said. Lucy had always slept in Eric's room. The moorhen, recovering from a broken leg, was in a box of hay in the kitchen. She was restive and not at all happy with the move. I did my best to soothe her.

'Now come along, eat your nice dinner and stop fussing,' I said, half covering her box and making her comfortable. 'Oh dear, now look what you've done in your water-bowl!' Moorhens have a habit of using their water-bowls as lavatories . . .

So my bedsit bird hospital became the Chalet bird hospital and a very busy day was over. The hospital was run by me, single-handed; Eric took no part – he had other, very different interests. He didn't even particularly like birds, though he grew fond of some of my patients: Wol, in particular.

That night I lay in bed almost hemmed in by cages; Clara's Cage was only two feet away and Wol's actually touching the foot of my bed. My bed was down the very narrow part of the sitting-room, the head of the bed against a north-facing window which overlooked our small garden and the big garden over the fence. Actually, this narrow part had once been a sort of lean-to shed that had been added on. Directly outside the window was a square concrete coal-bunker, which was at the end of the concrete 'patio'. The kitchen also faced north and had the same view. The opposite end of the sitting-room was the south window; this looked on to a small lawn and large tarmac car-park; beyond was the main road.

The Chalet rooms were all linked; you stepped in through the door from the patio, turning right for the kitchen and left into the sitting-room. Walking the length of the latter, a door to the right led into Eric's bedroom, then through two close-together doors into the tiny bathroom. There was a bath and a loo in here – no room for any wash-basin. Possibly its only redeeming feature was a nice view down the side of the building across the garden and fields.

And that was it . . . our new home.

So I lay in bed and stared at the ceiling, planning the little duck-pen and pond I was going to make for Lucy down one end of our new little garden. She'd never had a pond to swim on – only various basins to bathe in in my old room. And tomorrow I'd fix that high perch Wol favoured across an angle of the room, over Crusoe's cage; he'd like that. He was out in the room most of the day, now, usually only confined to a cage at night.

Eventually I fell asleep, counting birds, not sheep; last year I'd treated 164 – the most ever. How many would be brought me this year, I wondered.

2

Feathered Friends and Creepy-Crawlies

*T*he next few days were fairly action-packed. Outside I'd been digging what I hoped would eventually be a flower-bed, and I'd made Lucy a little duck-pen one end. It was about nine feet square and Eric had helped me to make a small duck-house under the hedge which bordered one side of the pen. Part of the wooden fence formed the second side, and I made an eighteen inches high Twilweld fence for the other two sides of the square; this latter was so I could step into and out of the pen easily. What would I do without Twilweld? I should have bought shares in the stuff years ago. I hadn't got down to making her a pond yet but she had the large rectangular Polythene bath filled with water to splash and bathe in. The bath had proved very useful on many occasions in the past.

Three cages were stacked neatly in the kitchen, squeezed in between a fridge and the recently painted but ancient monument that was laughingly called a kitchen cabinet. The latter must have come out of the Ark, we decided; the bottom right-hand corner smelled so strongly of tom-cat pee that I'd had to scrub and disinfect it not once but about four times, sploshing Jeyes Fluid around in undiluted form. There were gaps and flaking hardboard throughout the cupboard space and silver-fish were having a ball, scurrying around the damp, fusty interior. There was a great deal of cleaning involved before I dared put anything inside.

I'd also fixed up Wol's perch over the chest-of-drawers, as promised, and by evening of the second day he was perched up there watching the television inside and the traffic going down the main road outside. The tawny owl had always been a telly addict, right

13

from a small owlet, but now he had the cars to watch and this he found equally fascinating.

Soon it was business as usual.

Three days after we moved in someone brought me an injured robin fledgling.

'Oh, is it a robin?' the girl asked. 'We thought it was a little thrush.'

I put the pretty little speckled bird in a handy budgie cage and placed it on top of the electric cooker. I hadn't quite finished the small top cage of the three stacked ones; later, it would come in very useful for small birds and fledglings. The other two cages were soon known to me as the Upper Duck Cage and the Lower Duck Cage though any smaller birds would be all right in them and perches could easily be fixed across. These latter two cages were made of wood, hardboard and Twilweld (of course!), as were Katy's cage and two others I had; the rest were cardboard – with Twilweld doors. All made by me.

I fed the robin morsels of raw mince with my scissor-type eyebrow tweezers (I'd found these invaluable and had several pairs) and he opened his beak obligingly each time, making the familar 'tseee-tseee' noise – rather like hissing through almost-but-not-quite clenched teeth – before accepting each piece. You hear this noise frequently in a garden where robins have been nesting in the springtime. As well as raw mince, the little robin took a great liking to scrambled egg and also bread-and-milk. I half covered the budgie cage – no wild bird likes to be too exposed – and he settled down to snooze on one of the several twiggy perches provided.

Several young blackbirds later, I was called out to collect a swift that had apparently crash-landed in someone's garden. He seemed unhurt but I decided to keep the bird overnight; by the morning I believed he'd be ready for release. It is almost impossible for a swift to take off from the ground because of tiny short legs and long tapered wings. Designed for flight and spending the best part of their lives in the air, they will die unless helped. But, oh dear, in the past I'd usually released swifts from the top bathroom of the tall old house; from there they could swoop clear of trees and other buildings. But now there was no top bathroom.

'I wonder what I'd better do?' I said to Eric at lunchtime.

'Your problem,' he mumbled over a cheese-and-pickle sandwich. 'You're the expert.'

'Hmm. Well I suppose I'd better take him up the hill.'

I didn't feel much like a longish uphill walk, but I'd already delayed his release to the afternoon and I couldn't put it off any longer, so I put the swift in one of my much-used square hat-boxes and set off down the garden to walk the length of the twenty-two-acre field, the bottom side of which bordered the garden. The last part of my trek consisted of a fairly steep climb to the lane which ran across the top, then through a gate, across the lane and a further climb up a narrow path alongside another field towards the large Elizabethan mansion beyond, which was my destination. I had discovered that the wall at the bottom of the terrace there was an ideal place for releasing swifts and house-martins; facing south, there was a magnificent view of the surrounding countryside, the land in front dropping sharply away and sloping down the way I'd come.

'Off you go!' I said, throwing the little swift into the air as I leaned over the wall. 'Take care of yourself now.'

He soared into the air from my hands, turning in wide circles and gaining height until he was just a speck in the sky, eventually disappearing from sight. I heaved a sigh of relief. There was always the chance he might have crash-landed again and perhaps got lost; after all, why had he done so the previous day in someone's garden? But he'd flown perfectly.

I walked back slowly pondering on the strange lifestyle of swifts in general. It would probably be years before the little bird I'd released landed again and then it would most likely only be to nest and raise a family. If all went well. They were supposed even to sleep on the wing; being an insomniac and having great difficulty in sleeping even in a comfortable bed, my mind boggled at the thought. I trudged on. Grazing ponies lifted their heads and stared at me. 'Has she got something nice to eat in that box she's carrying? Better go and see.' Some of them walked towards me.

Back home there were mouths to feed: blackbird and starling fledglings were coming in almost daily; mainly cat victims. We were on the telephone now and it seldom seemed to stop ringing. 'My cat's just caught a little thrush – could I bring it over?' Invariably, in fact nine times out of ten, 'little thrushes' turned out to be little blackbirds. It surprised me that so few people seemed to know the difference, thinking only that a blackbird had to be black and a thrush was supposed to be speckled. For the benefit of anyone still confused here it is: a male blackbird is black with a yellow beak, the female being a dark brown with a brownish beak. A young blackbird fledgling is brown – sometimes quite light, sometimes dark – with lighter coloured speckles on the breast. Male and female song-thrushes are identical and so are their off-spring: brown backs and cream coloured breasts with dark speckles. There – now you know! Robins, of course, have red breasts but their youngsters are brown and speckled very like a blackbird fledgling. But much smaller, of course: robin size.

The Chalet had been empty for about a year before we came; that is, empty of human occupants. I once read somewhere that, if not controlled, insects would take over the world. During those first weeks we were to discover that they hadn't yet taken over the world but they'd made a start: they'd taken over the Chalet. The silver-fish in the kitchen cabinet weren't the only creatures having a ball; large, orangey-coloured slugs appeared nightly in the bathroom and one or two woodlice were lumbering up the wall a few inches from my head. Woodlice are fine, in their place, but I was afraid these fellows might lose their footing and end up in bed with me, so I caught them and put them outside. Now I can get on with spiders, mice, rats and even snakes, at a pinch, but slugs have always given me the creeps. And these orange monsters were the largest I'd ever seen; solitary ones slithered silently up the walls near the loo while others peeped out slugily (slugishly?) from under the cracks round the bath. Horrified, I rushed for Eric each time; he was very good at slug disposal.

'Quick – there's another one! There ... there!' I shrieked, cowering in the background.

'All right, all right – leave it to me,' he'd say, and I was only too glad to do so. Ugh!

It got so I'd cautiously open the bathroom door in the evening, switch on the light with trembling hand and peer into the room before entering. Even then one couldn't be sure; what was that behind the bathroom door? Oh, no!

'Darling!'

'Not *another?*'

This went on for some months. We blocked up cracks and small holes with Polyfilla but still the occasional slug broke through the defences.

'I think they must be coming from under the bath,' Eric announced one day. He went outside and blocked round the drain and pipe entrances. 'There – that should fix them.'

But it didn't. Those slugs were determined characters; as far as they were concerned the bathroom was theirs and probably had been for the past twelve months ...

I used to dread the evenings; having a weak bladder I was in and out the dreaded bathroom a good deal; one cup of tea and it was off to Slugland. I was glad the birds, so feathery and charming, took my mind off slithery things during the daylight hours.

3

Lucy and the Eggs

*W*ol was obviously enjoying our new home. The cars on the main road absolutely fascinated him – better than telly, even – and sometimes he flew across the room to the window to have a closer look, and, head rotating madly, he'd perch there with his eyes glued on the movement outside; having led a sheltered life, I don't suppose he'd ever seen a car before. He liked movement; as an owlet his taste on the television had usually run to cowboys and Indians or cops and robbers – the latter with plenty of car chases. He was definitely a James Bond fan, was Wol.

Crusoe wasn't so sure about the change. He'd been looking rather disgruntled; crows are good at this. As the weather improved I took to putting him outside on the ivy-covered stump near the duck-pen and he took a great fancy to perching up there, watching everything. There was an elder tree growing at the back which gave him some shelter – he didn't like being too exposed – and he sometimes climbed on to a low branch of that. Unable to fly because of an old wing injury, the crow sometimes sprang off the five-foot-high stump to explore either the thicket beyond or the concrete patio in front of the Chalet. He'd strut around on the latter with his funny gammy-leg walk (he had an arthriticky leg as well but a course of Cortisone had made it much better) and poke his beak into anything that took his fancy. In the summer, my newly planted flowers took his fancy; crows are dreadfully destructive and he took a fiendish delight in pulling up small plants or pecking them to pieces – or pulling off the petals.

'That's the last time I buy you any petunias/pansies/antirrhinums,' Eric would exclaim, aghast at such wilful destruction. 'That bloody crow's a menace!'

I was inclined to agree; I loved my flowers and I used to get really mad at Crusoe.

'Shut him up – take him inside!' would be the next roar.

'But he loves it out here – I'll put him up on the tree stump again.'

But Eric wasn't to be deterred. 'Look at those pansies – waste of money buying them!' He bent down and glared at their poor mangled petals.

'Crusoe – don't you dare do that again,' I threatened, wagging a finger at him sternly as he poked around in the ivy on the stump, looking the picture of innocence. But of course, being a crow, he did – again and again. If I covered the delicate plants with a piece of wire-netting he removed it with the flick of a beak and if I put stakes round the plant he removed each one of these too, usually carrying them to his water-bowl. Crows love to put things in water; sometimes I'd find poor drowned worms, pale and still or feebly wriggling at the bottom of my awful crow's bowl. He liked to pull up worms and often did, but I never saw him actually eat one.

Meanwhile, Lucy had been acting strangely for the past few days. Restless and quacky, she seemed ill at ease. Then, one morning when I went to lift her out of the box in Eric's room she didn't want to move.

'Come along, Lucy – what's the matter? Oh . . .'

The matter was she'd laid an egg – her very first! And she wanted to sit on it.

'Oh, well . . . all right.' I left her to it.

'Why's Lucy still in her sleeping box?' enquired Eric at lunchtime as he sat on the bed changing his shoes. He hadn't noticed earlier.

'She's sitting on an egg.'

'Egg – what egg?' He stopped in mid-shoe and stared, frowning.

'She laid one last night, or rather, I expect it was early this morning,' I answered. 'I was going to put her outside but she wanted to sit on it.'

'Hmmph,' said Eric. His hmmph sounded pretty non-committal so I hoped for the best.

In between scurrying about after all the birds I was doing the usual chores, but now and again I paused to smile benignly at Lucy. I'd never had an egg-laying duck before. And I hadn't yet learnt that, as with egg-laying hens, one merely took each egg that was laid away and let the hen or duck go about its business. In my naivety I just hadn't liked to part my Lucy from her egg. But if I'd been less soft-hearted (stupid?) I'd have saved myself a lot of trouble. Because I soon discovered that Lucy the duck made the most dreadful smelly messes during her egg-laying and sitting activities.

'Phew!' exclaimed Eric early next morning, accepting the cup of tea I handed him. 'There's a *dreadful* smell coming from Lucy's box;

for goodness sake *do* something.'

He was quite right – there was. It was putrid . . . a really awful pong. I peered inside. Lucy was now sitting glassy-eyed on two eggs. Birds seem to go into a sort of trance when sitting on eggs, I reflected; all birds.

'All right, all right – I'll give her box a good clean out,' I said quickly.

I removed Lucy and eggs and all the bedding, then I sloshed around with a lot of strong disinfectant, putting in layers of clean newspaper and a nice straw bed afterwards. I lifted duck and eggs back into the box again.

'There – she's nice and clean again now. No smell.'

A couple of hours later – thankfully after Eric had gone to work – Lucy let rip again . . .

It went on for days – or was it weeks? – me feverishly cleaning, Lucy laying eggs and making fearful pongs. I was so afraid Eric would banish Lucy from his room that I daren't let up.

One day I found Eric bending over the box staring thoughtfully at the motionless duck on her nest.

'We're not going to have ducklings all over the place, are we?' he enquired, turning round.

'No . . . no, of course not,' I answered hurriedly. 'They're not fertile.'

'Oh . . . no, of course they wouldn't be,' he said, relieved. He wandered off.

Little did he know, however, how this had set me thinking; it did seem an awful shame for Lucy to sit in vain. After all, she must fancy being a mum; she must *think* she was going to be one? That's what it was all about.

I rang Pam. 'Pam, you don't happen to have any fertile duck eggs, do you?' I explained the situation. Pam usually had a variety of ducks and drakes.

'Well, let me see . . . mmm, yes, I can let you have a couple of Khaki Campbell eggs. Haven't any mallard ones I'm sure of, though.'

'Fine – thanks, I'll come right over.'

'The father was a white Aylesbury drake called Henry,' Pam told me when I arrived to collect the eggs. She was always a mine of information. 'He used to be on that stream near the Library before he came to me.' She handed me the two eggs carefully wrapped in cotton-wool and still warm. 'They should hatch all right,' she added.

I drove home feeling quite excited and slipped the eggs under Lucy, removing two of hers. She was now trying to incubate about six. She sat stoically on, never batting a little round eyelid. But what would Eric say? I'd cross that bridge when I came to it; after all, they might not hatch . . .

Once a year – and *only* once – I donned the old glad rags and went to Royal Ascot races with my sister, who called for me. It was this very morning that Lucy hatched one of her eggs. Tiny duckling noises emerged from under her and there was a pretty little dark-brown duckling with a pale cream front! I was thrilled – and so, I think, was Lucy. After all those weeks of sitting!

'Isn't it *sweet*?' I said to Eric.

'I thought you said they weren't going to hatch?' said he, frowning and less enthusiastic. Well, I'd *meant* to tell him.

How could I bear to leave the new duckling – even for five minutes? It *would* have to be the day we were going to Ascot.

'Look, isn't it *gorgeous*?' I said to my sister when she arrived an hour later, dressed up to the nines and in the usual hurry.

'Mm . . . yes, very pretty. Now hurry up, we'd better get going or we'll never find anywhere to park.'

I wanted to go to the races . . . but I hated leaving the new arrival. I had one last look . . .

'*Do* hurry up,' said my sister. 'Now, have you got everything? Good-bye, Eric,' and she was halfway down the garden path with me bringing up the rear carrying two hat-boxes – containing baby birds, not hats! – and my posh Ascot hat.

On the way we stopped at Pam's; she was going to feed the young fledglings while we were away and I was to collect them on the way home. Pam had been a tower of strength over the years, giving help, advice and comfort when needed, as had her son, Steve, who was now a qualified vet and marvellous with birds.

Eric was keeping an eye on the other birds back home; at least, I hoped he was. It only happened once a year.

During the afternoon, in between admiring the horses, studying the fashions and backing losers, I found myself day-dreaming about the new baby duckling.

'What? . . . oh, sorry . . . what did you say?'

'I said, which one do you fancy?' asked my sister leaning on the rails of the paddock. It was all right for her; as a farmer's wife she was used to things coming out of eggs.

Back home – my feet were killing me – I dashed in to see Lucy. Mother and child were just fine; I don't think they'd noticed my absence.

Lucy sat determinedly on the second of Pam's eggs for quite some time but this one failed to hatch. The rest of her clutch I'd had to remove as they'd become addled. But at least she had one duckling.

4

A Floppy Drake
and a Cuckoo

*L*ucy's duckling seemed to grow at an amazing rate: a month after hatching he was about twice her size and a month later I reckoned he was three times the size of his rather small – Lucy *was* rather small, smaller than an ordinary mallard – foster mum. He was nigger-brown with a creamy-white shirt front and matching outer flight feathers: extremely handsome! I called him Bean Bag after the ones people sit on because Bean was incredibly floppy. He liked sitting on my lap and the occasional cuddle – he was soppy as well as floppy – and he seemed to relax so completely that it felt as if he'd no bones in his body. If I held my hands low down, fingers interlaced, he's step on to them to climb up on to my knee: up I go, now . . . flop! He felt more like a lump of dough, I used to think, than a large bony drake. Like all the drakes I've ever reared he enjoyed twining his neck round mine while I held his body against my chest, his legs hanging down, and would close his eyes in bliss when I fondled his neck.

I might mention here that whereas drakes appear to enjoy all this sort of thing, ducks do not. Mostly the latter get quacky and slightly hysterical at the very thought of close encounters of the human kind. Couldn't be more different.

Bean Bag also liked me to stroke his webbed feet and would lay his beak in my other proffered hand and apparently go into a sort of trance. He also enjoyed nibbling ears and fiddling with strands of hair; memories of Wol Owl, who also enjoyed hair-fiddling in his youth.

When Bean Bag wasn't being a soppy drake he was outside in the duck-pen with Lucy. He spent most of each day out there, as he had done from a few days old. Lucy was still very fond of her enormous foster son and they got on very well together. Watching them pottering around in there one day I decided it was high time I dug them a proper pond. So I got digging. It was hard work as the soil was heavy and sticky; I'd decided it must be in the very corner of the pen to save space and this, too, made excavating even more difficult. When it was finished the pond was rectangular and was about four feet long, two feet wide and eighteen inches deep. Then I had to manipulate the stiff pond-liner into position, making sure there was a good overlap, and arrange what I call 'flat bricks' – sometimes used for garden paths – around the edge to keep the liner in place. I had to cut the latter to the right size and I got in a terrible mess with the unwieldly corners, but at last it was finished; now for the water. Fortunately there was a tap just near by, so I fixed up the hose – it only *just* reached – and there it was: a pond! Not very large, it's true, but deep enough, it proved, for ducks to even swim around under water.

Lucy and Bean Bag eyed it with suspicion at first but soon got the message. First Lucy slid on to the water and had a good bathe and then, when she eventually climbed out, Bean Bag jumped in. Afterwards they both stood on the brick edge and preened . . .

'I see you've made them a pond,' remarked Eric, arriving home early evening. 'Looks quite nice.'

But I was lying flat out on my back on the bed, exhausted, and scarcely heard him.

'Any tea? What's for supper?' he asked my prostrate body.

I was too tired even to lift an arm and throw a cushion at him.

Late November our handsome drake flew away. It had been a stormy, blustery day and just before dusk Bean Bag stood in the duck-pen, head up, neck outstretched, facing into the strong wind. Suddenly, without warning, he took off, gaining height rapidly. Flying due west, he quickly disappeared from view in spite of my yell, 'Bean . . . come back!' It was getting darker and stormier by the minute; what a time to choose for a maiden flight.

Sadly, we never saw him again. Lucy, I'm convinced, was as shaken and surprised as I was; Eric was out at the time but was equally surprised when I told him later. Next day I searched by the river and made enquiries but nobody had seen him and I couldn't find him anywhere.

Lucy was very quiet for a few days and I could tell that Bean Bag's sudden departure had upset her. They'd seemed so happy together and he hadn't appeared at all restless or given any indication that he was about to fly off. No doubt he'd gone to explore pastures new, however, and we could only wish him well and hope that he'd be happy, wherever he was . . .

Some time later Pam let me have a little mallard drake she'd hand-reared as a mate for Lucy. But it was not a success. Lucy hated him. She pecked and chased the poor chap mercilessly and I could see it was never going to work; no way was she going to have this stranger in her duck-pen. So he had to go back.

Actually, my matchmaking efforts had seldom been successful. Young lady blackbirds introduced to what I took to be lonely male blackbirds were invariably subjected to great harassment and ferocious pecking attacks and usually had to be removed while they still had a feather left. On the whole, I found blackbird patients preferred to share a cage with song-thrushes, for example, rather than with the opposite sex of their own species. And of course one could never put two male blackbirds in the same cage, however roomy, or they'd fight like tigers.

One or two amusing things had happened that summer. The robin, my first patient in the Chalet, had long since flown but we still saw him around. He seemed to know us and be doing fine. Sam, a young starling I'd reared and who had moved to our new home with us was still around, too, and was very tame. He was mad about bread-and-milk, starlings usually are, and weeks after release still came in and out the kitchen for it, helping himself from a dish on the table (though if I were around he expected me to feed him). Sam also had the habit of coming into the sitting-room to take a nap in Clara's Cage, near my bed, Chloe and Bully, the two finches, having been moved. Outside on the patio Sam sometimes perched on my head if I relaxed in a deck-chair reading a newspaper, or even jumped on the paper itself, and he partook of frequent very splashy baths in a large flower-pot saucer nearby. One day he appeared from nowhere and actually landed on the rim of a hot cup of tea I was holding, dipping his beak in the liquid and appearing to take a quick drink before flying away again. I was amazed at this latest antic; that tea was really hot.

Sam was around for four months, gradually appearing less and less. When he last appeared in the autumn he'd grown into a handsome bird with shining winter plumage. His mother had been tragically killed by a fish-hook lodged in her throat and young Sam very nearly died of exposure when still a naked and blind baby. I was pleased he'd made it; his mother, I felt, would have been proud of him.

A little sparrow I had amused me, too. She'd been thrown out of her nest by some house-martins, I was told: this sometimes happens. She was reared in the usual way and eventually released, but like Sam – and others – frequently returned for bread-and-milk. We also saw quite a lot of her outside. One afternoon I was standing on the patio eating a honey sandwich. I held the sandwich up to my mouth and was just about to take a bite when the sparrow flew across, and, hovering in front of me like an outsize humming-bird, pecked a piece out of it and then flew off to join the other sparrows in the nearby lilac bushes. It all happened so quickly I could scarcely believe it. But there was the neat beak-shaped bite out of my sandwich to prove it.

Early one morning three children in riding clothes handed me a young cuckoo. I was delighted: I'd never had a cuckoo before.

'We found him in the driveway,' one of them said. 'He was just standing on the gravel at the side looking very forlorn.'

The cuckoo fledgling was very hungry and opened his enormous mouth for food. It was bright orange in colour and I could well imagine how busy some unfortunate little foster mum must have been keeping pace with his appetite faced with that gape all day long. She was probably glad to have got shot of him. However, it was now up to me to carry on where she left off, it seemed. I put the cuckoo in the lower two-thirds of the wooden cage near the bottom of my bed; the one Wol used to be in. The latter was now the other side of the room, and the top third of the cage – it had been divided up – was now occupied by the two finches. I had used a Daler board to divide the cage, kept in place with paperclip 'hooks'.

Now cuckoos may have a bad reputation but this youngster was a real charmer. Browny/grey with a barred front, he was well behaved, friendly and quite unafraid. His legs were a trifle wobbly at first but regular drops of Abidec – a concentrated liquid form of vitamins – soon made them stronger. He had no tail to speak of and it was to be five months before he grew a proper one, for some reason. His favourite food was egg of any kind, but he accepted bits of most things including the ever-popular Go Cat, bread-and-milk and mealworms. He never liked the raw minced steak that blackbirds and many other birds loved.

Cucky Boy, as we called him, took a great interest in everything going on in the room. He loved being in the sun and I fixed up a special perch for him across the south facing window of the room; I often let him out of his cage and he'd fly over there whenever it was sunny and perch contentedly, watching the cars go by and enjoying the warmth. Of course, when the cuckoo was out in the room, Wol had to be firmly shut in his cage, and vice versa: an owl-and-cuckoo fight was definitely *not* on the cards. Wol made it clear he didn't think much of Cucky Boy; he'd stare across at him rather disdainfully, then, blinking, turn away.

After eight days and a large amount of food stuffed down his throat, Cucky learnt to feed himself. It was a great relief. Sometimes he came into the kitchen, perching on the sill and looking across the

Cucky.

north side of the garden or perching on the kettle – unlike Wol he seemed to prefer the kettle to the teapot – and watching me do the chores. He was never any trouble to catch and would perch on my hand as tame as a budgie. He was a placid bird, surveying everything with a look of almost child-like innocence and seeming to be content to accept anything that befell him with very good grace. I would describe him as a nice bird; we were both very fond of our cuckoo.

The Amorous Pigeon

One day Pam and a friend of hers brought me four baby coots. Apparently the latter had found them drowning on the river near her home. I forget why Pam palmed them off on me; I think she may have been going away for a few days, or maybe she just thought I'd like some baby coots to rear.

I wasn't too pleased, actually, having learnt through bitter experience that whereas baby moorhens were very sweet, co-operative and could even be house-trained, coot chicks were the exact opposite: difficult, unobliging and extremely messy. Eric used to ask – after listening to a one-sided telephone conversation – 'It's a *moorhen* chick, is it? Not one of those ruddy coots?'

However, I made the four little coots comfortable with the usual warm hot-water bottle in a box of hay and then fed them a stiff mixture of Farex baby food, which they pecked from the end of a yellow plastic spoon: that is, three of them took the food, the fourth refusing not only the Farex but everything else offered. It was the smallest and weakest of the four and never really looked like surviving, though I did my best to save the little thing. It died two days later. But the others did well and were even quite co–operative, in spite of all my misgivings. They were comical little things with their black woolly bodies, rust-coloured wiry 'hair' round the neck and head, and white tip to their tiny red beaks. They kept up a plaintive cry most of the time – coot chicks do – and Eric wasn't too pleased.

'Those bloody coot chicks . . . don't they ever shut up?' he wanted to know. 'Put them in the bathroom!'

But when I tried this the cries rose to a crescendo; they didn't think much of it in there.

26

Very soon the triplets scorned Farex, wanting only meat; preferably the very best and most expensive finely minced steak. Later, thankfully, they went mad on tinned cat food: Choosy with Cod.

After about two weeks I partitioned off part of the duck-pen for them, where they dashed up and down on rubbery lobed feet and paddled in a shallow dish. The latter was a cat litter-tray made of Polythene; I found these ideal for small water-birds to paddle in.

About this time, Pinky came to stay. He was a feral pigeon found in the town with a broken leg. The leg was taped up and set well and it wasn't long before he was limping around outside, then flying and quite normal again. But he didn't fly away, oh dear no. Pigeons know a good thing when they see one; Pinky had a comfortable place in which to roost at night and corn to eat during the day: why go anywhere else?

I had put two box cages on top of the kitchen-cabinet; they had the usual Twilweld wire doors which opened downwards or were fixed into place with the usual 'hook' – a paper-clip – and Pinky had taken over one of these.

Now he was a very sexy pigeon – even more so than most – and nothing with two legs and feathers was safe from his advances. He had many visiting girlfriends but Pinky obviously believed in variety being the spice of life and one morning he flew down from the Chalet roof and tried to mate with one of the young coots, now half-grown and sharing the whole duck-pen with Lucy. Their shrill cries of protest brought me running outside just in time to see the awful Pinky disappear into the duck-house in hot pursuit of his intended. There were a lot more cries and scuffling before I managed to drag him out.

'Pinky . . . you're dreadful!' I scolded. 'Don't you *dare* do that again!' But he did; whenever my back was turned.

The nicely brought up young lady coots were terrified, but Pinky was determined. Whether it was always the same one he chose I wasn't sure – they all looked alike. Lucy remained aloof and totally uninterested, while all this was going on. It was a relief all round when after a few days Pinky found himself a new pigeon girlfriend.

'You know what *that* bird needs, don't you?' said Eric one day, stabbing a finger meaningfully in the general direction of our local Romeo. 'De—' But I won't go into this further.

Pinky's new amour was a fairly new patient of mine called Ponky. She was another feral pigeon, brought to me one day dripping with water.

'What happened?' I asked the damp-looking girl clutching her.

'I found it in the Grand Union Canal at Southall,' was the reply. 'Don't know how it fell in.'

It seemed a funny place to find a pigeon, but these things happen.

Ponky soon recovered and Pinky lost no time in courting her, puffing himself out and strutting in front of her with amorous coos her first day outside.

The coots celebrated their new-found peace by climbing up the wire-netting at the back of the duck-pen and disappearing in the now dense undergrowth beyond. The nettles there were nearly five feet high and there were old fallen trees and a positive network of brambles and thick ivy everywhere, as well as trees. It took me hours to find the miscreants and after I'd returned them to the pen they promptly climbed right out again almost before I'd got my breath back, and I had to start clambering around after them all over again; it was surprising how fast they could move considering their lobed feet were hardly designed for this purpose.

I decided the time had come to get them on the lake; not the one across the big field surrounded by woods but a privately owned lake about a mile away that belonged to a lady I knew. It was a beautiful lake with weeping willows dipping over the water and woods all around. In the middle there was a floating platform and wooden duck-house which was very popular with the mallards and other waterfowl that flew to and fro the nearby river. Every day this lady called, 'Quack. .ers!' from outside her kitchen door, throwing bread on to the sloping lawn and the ducks swam towards her, clambered out of the water and waddled up to be fed.

I took the three young coots there in a box and they swam away quite happily and soon settled down. I knew they'd be just fine. I took all the ducklings I reared to this lake now as soon as they were able to fly and fend for themselves: usually around eight weeks old. It was a lovely place for them and seemed more peaceful than the river. Bean Bag would probably have gone there eventually, had he stayed.

Meanwhile Pinky's would-be mate had deserted him for another young male, and he had a new girlfriend misnamed Duggie (I'd thought it was another male, but Pinky soon put me wise). Duggie was a racing pigeon; a not very successful racing pigeon who was in the habit of getting lost and whose owner had decided he didn't want her back. I could keep her, he said. So out on the patio she met up with the amorous Pinky, who wasted no time at all in courting her, his umpteenth girlfriend.

Two months later he started making a nest.

'What was *that*?' cried Eric, his eyes screwed up as he bent over the kitchen sink, washing.

'Er, what do you mean?'

He straightened up, wiping his face on a towel.

'Something touched my head . . . there! It's that damn pigeon!

It's got a stick or something . . . what's going on?' He glared up at the cage on the kitchen cabinet. 'It's that bloody Pinky!'

I'd been rather dreading Eric's morning ablutions because for the past hour Pinky had been flying frantically in and out of the kitchen window with small twigs. Some of them weren't all that small, either, and it was one of the longer ones that had brushed Eric's head.

'He's . . . er . . building a nest,' I murmured weakly.

'A nest? Where? Not up *there*?' He indicated Pinky's box, frowning and aghast.

'Well, yes.'

'Oh, *no* . . . we can't have pigeons nesting in the kitchen,' my husband groaned. 'It's bad enough him being up there at all.'

'Well, I thought it was rather sweet, really. And it won't do any harm up there out of the way,' I soothed, without conviction.

Eric ducked as another twig whistled past. I'd been side-stepping and ducking since the operation started when I first opened the window and went into the kitchen to make the early morning tea.

Eric slammed the window shut, muttered something unprintable and stalked out of the kitchen in a huff. Pinky, twig in beak, was standing on the little platform outside and to the right of the window. The latter had originally been designed for milk bottles but birds flying in and out found it very useful.

I opened the window again . . .

It took Pinky four days to complete the very untidy nest of twigs in one corner of his box cage. Duggie took no part in this building operation but went to inspect it when the nest was finished and apparently approved, laying her first egg up there four days later. Two days after that she laid the second egg: pigeons always lay just two eggs. Then the incubating started, Pinky taking the day shift and Duggie taking over at night.

Things were pretty quiet in the kitchen during this period as each pigeon took it in turns, motionless, on the eggs. Being high up, fortunately, Eric couldn't actually see into the cage and I hoped he'd forgotten about the whole thing. I had to stand on the stool to see.

After sixteen days the first little pigeon chick hatched early one morning; the second, that afternoon. Duggie carefully removed the empty pieces of shell each time, throwing them out on to the kitchen floor. I stood on the high stool and smiled at the two squirming babies.

'Aah!'

My smiles were short lived, however, because soon there was trouble: the pigeons brooding made a terrible mess up there; all over the tangled stick nest.

'Pooh!' said Eric a few days later, wrinkling his nose. 'What a *smell*!'

Memories of Lucy . . .

'Well, I haven't liked to clean it out for fear of them deserting the babies,' I said truthfully. I agreed with him, though, that something would have to be done soon: it *did* stink and it wasn't very hygienic in the kitchen. So one morning I stood on the stool and carefully removed the soiled newspaper from under the nest and cleaned up a bit, disturbing the two nestlings as little as possible. Both parent birds happened to be out at the time.

Within two days, though, both baby pigeons were dead and I felt awful: was it all my fault? Pinky and Duggie had returned to the nest all right after the cleaning and had presumably continued feeding their youngsters, but . . . well, I could see they hadn't been too pleased with my interference.

I cleaned out the whole awful mess in Pinky's cage again and thoroughly disinfected it, thinking rather sadly that that was that. But a week later Pinky started a new nest and the whole thing started again.

'Oh, no . . . not *again*?' Eric stared in disbelief as a twig flashed past. I don't *believe* it!'

'I'm afraid so.'

But the second set of twins died too. Shortly after hatching Duggie disappeared. While its mate was on the nest the other pigeon often went for a fly around the field. This particular morning Duggie set off and was never seen again. We suspected she might have been shot; we often heard shots being fired in the big field and there'd been shooting that morning. Certainly no female would desert her newly hatched chicks and mate unless something had happened to her. I felt very sad indeed about it: Pinky tried to rear the babies on his own but, seeing them grow weaker, I attempted to help with drops of Farex. But it was no use.

I felt sorry for Pinky, too. He and Duggie had seemed so devoted. But three months later he found himself a new mate.

6

Albert Comes to Stay

*E*arly in the New Year three youngsters had brought me a heron. They said they'd found him in a field near a cutting of the river and said he'd been just crouching there in the cold, looking hungry and dejected. And it was cold, too; we were in the grips of some really freezing weather with snow and ice everywhere. It was a hard time for all wild creatures.

This heron – I called him Harold – was only a youngster. He appeared unhurt but desperately hungry, so I installed him in the large duck-cage vacated by Bean Bag at the bottom of my bed and set about feeding him. It was a Sunday of course (why do I always get birds requiring special food – like a hawk or fish-eating bird – on a Sunday?) and so, not having a deep-freeze or anything, the best I could do was Farex and soaked Go Cat, which he accepted gladly. Next day Eric got me some of the frozen packs of very large sardines – the size of small herrings – which were greatly favoured by another heron I once had. Each night I thawed out enough for the next day; the packs just fitted into the rather small freezer compartment of our rather small, no-room-for-a-larger-one fridge. Two days later Eric managed to get Harold some fresh sprats as well – the heron had a very healthy appetite – and in between times he was knocking back large beakfuls of Salmon Go Cat (now, sadly, unobtainable) and eating this also at night.

He was a friendly chap and I have a note here which says he 'enjoyed his thighs and tummy stroked'! He grew strong and fit again fairly quickly, and after two weeks we took him to a place where he would be re-habilitated, prior to release. He was a nice bird, but, like all herons, very expensive to feed, and it was something of a relief when he was able to depart. And when my room was free of fishy smells once more.

Soon after Harold left, a lady I knew brought round a really awkward customer: a great crested grebe.

'An Irishman handed him in to me in a plastic bag,' she said. 'It was at twenty past eight this morning,' she added. 'Can you take him?' She said she didn't know where the chap with the plastic bag had found the bird.

History looked like repeating itself – I'd had trouble with one of these birds before.

The grebe was bleeding from a small wound at the side of his breast, so I bathed this and fixed him up in a fairly large rectangular box I'd acquired on a comfortable bed of straw. He didn't seem at all troubled by this injury and I decided it was only superficial and would soon heal. Tiger, as I very soon and aptly named him, was one of the fiercest birds I'd ever had. He went out of his way to stab at me with his dagger-like bill at every possible opportunity. The second I opened the wire top flap of his box to put in food or water he'd make a mad dash at my hand, pecking it viciously and repeatedly. He also struggled violently when handled, scolding me with sharp 'barking' noises, and was a most difficult bird in every respect. He refused to pick up any food so I had to forcibly feed him slivers of sardine, getting badly pecked for my trouble.

Mercifully for both of us, Tiger's small wound healed well, and on the fourth day I was able to carry him in a box – kicking and struggling violently – to the river. Immediately he swam to the very middle of the swiftly flowing Thames and allowed himself to drift downstream, head held high and glancing neither to the right nor left. Twice he dived, quickly reappearing, and soon disappeared from sight. Somehow he kept up his arrogant disapproval of my handling and the whole episode right to the end.

I hate to say it, but he really was a most unpleasant character. My hands were covered in painful peck marks, as invariably the grebe had drawn blood each time, and it was some weeks before the soreness went completely. It was my second fierce great crested grebe; I wasn't looking forward to a third.

Being near the river I got a good many water-birds brought me, especially baby mallard ducklings that were lost. But one day I got quite a surprise. It was early one evening on a cold March day when a girl I knew and her friends handed me a cardboard-box about eighteen inches high and a foot square.

'We found him drowning in the river,' said the girl. 'We were sitting on the bank when this man came through his garden gate, grumbling to himself, and tipped him into the water. There was a swift current and he nearly drowned.'

'Yes,' a boy with her confirmed. 'Chap muttered something about

Albert.

it hanging round his garden for several days. Honestly, he was horrible. Fancy doing a thing like that?'

While they were talking I'd set the box down and was undoing the flaps, eager to see the subject in question. And there, wet and shivering, was a white Indian Runner duck. His neck bent, because he was taller than the box, he looked the picture of misery as he regarded me with watery blue eyes. Quickly I gently lifted him out, thanking the youngsters for rescuing him. They'd had to wade in to reach him, they said, and one of them looked pretty wet himself.

'He doesn't seem to be injured,' I told them. 'He's just very cold and wet – and thin, too.'

They went off happily, knowing I loved ducks and he'd be in good hands. The girl had brought me several ducklings in the past that she'd rescued, living near the river as she did.

Now I'd never had an Indian Runner before, only having once seen one over at Pam's, and that was a brown one. I was delighted with Albert, as I christened him; it was love at first sight!

Drying him a bit with a towel, I brought him into the sitting-room and stood him on a newspaper in front of the fire. I sat in the armchair in front of it, one leg each side of the still shivering and very sad-looking drake to stop him waddling away. Not that Albert had any intention of moving, as it happened; enjoying the warmth, he stood quite still with steam rising off him as I spoke softly to him, fondling his head and neck as he blinked up at me. Standing up straight, he was about two feet tall. Later, when he'd dried off a little, I had him on my knee, soothing him until gradually the shivering stopped and he relaxed. I offered him food but the poor chap was too shocked and upset to eat that evening. I noticed one wing had been clipped and wondered who had done this and where he'd come from; and how old he was.

Eric was, of course, very surprised to see the 'new boy' when he came home later. 'Where did you get *that*?' he asked, throwing down his coat and peering at Albert. 'What *is* it? Doesn't look like an ordinary duck.'

And of course Indian Runners don't; they really are a very unusual shape. Among other things, they have been described as 'hock bottles on legs', having an upright stance, long neck and rectangular-shaped body with a leg on each bottom corner. Facing you, they look as if they haven't any wings as these are held behind and close to the body.

I explained how the young girl, Nicole, and her friends had found Albert.

'I see,' said Eric, then, 'where on earth are you going to put him? There's no room anywhere.'

'Yes, there is . . . in there.' I indicated the large cage just to the left as you entered the sitting-room door, underneath another large cage I usually put blackbirds in. It was large enough for me to get in – just about – and had the usual drop-down Twilweld front; when open, the cage looked like a small stable. 'He'll be fine in there.'

I made the new drake a thick, comfortable bed of straw and put in a big bowl of water and some food. He was dry and looked a bit happier now, but I'd filled him a large stone hot-water bottle so he'd be nice and warm after his traumatic experience on the choppy river. It was lucky the youngsters had been there to rescue him. It happened some miles away, and he'd have surely drowned if they'd not been at hand; Indian Runners aren't designed for rivers, being more of a farmyard duck.

'There you are, Albert,' I said as I lifted him into the box. 'You'll be all right now,' and I stroked his sleek white head. He stood there looking out until we went to bed, then I put up the wire door and half covered it; he could still stand up and look out across the room if he wanted to.

'Good night,' we both said, smiling on the new white drake as we went to bed. I could see Eric was going to be as fond of him as I already was; I knew I was hooked from the moment I undid the flaps of that box.

I was beaming at Albert next morning when a lorry drew up in the car-park and a man jumped out, hurrying towards the Chalet. He was carrying a small box in which there was an injured robin and a robin's egg in part of a nest.

'Found 'im in a garage – I was working in there, see, and this nest had been pulled down . . . cat or something.'

I thanked him for bringing the robin – he'd driven some thirty miles to reach me – and then I quickly made one of my famous home-made nests and popped the robin in this on a warm hot-water bottle. Poor little bird, she was very shocked and had a leg, breast and wing injury; in spite of all my efforts to save her, she died an hour later. I tried to incubate the little egg but the man had come a long way and it was cold when handed in. I was unsuccessful.

A sad little incident but one of many that happened during the spring and summer. Very many cat victims die through shock, if not their injuries. And it was obvious this little robin had suffered both, badly. The late Dorothy Yglesias of the famous Mousehole Bird Hospital and Sanctuary in Cornwall once wrote to me and said how well she knew the 'joy and sorrow' of wild bird hospital work: joy of seeing a bird restored to health and freedom; sorrow at one that fails to survive. And so it was all the time.

But there was never too much time to be sad, especially in the spring. There were always jobs to do and mouths to feed. Blackbird and starling fledglings were continually being brought to me; the former often jumped or were pushed from nests before they could fly properly and the latter seemed to make a habit of falling down chimneys or getting trapped in people's lofts. I usually put them in the topmost of the three cages stacked in the kitchen, feeding their ever-open beaks every two hours with small pieces of raw mince, soaked Go Cat or bread-and-milk; the younger ones getting Farex. If they had their way they'd be fed every twenty minutes, but only naked, baby chicks need feeding this often. One just had to turn a deaf ear to their cries; it was all too easy to overfeed and kill a fledgling, giving it food 'just to keep it quiet'. I'd made a sort of sliding door to this top and smallest of the three cages, which made it possible to close it a third, half or bit more. Frightened newcomers in particular liked to remain in the shadows.

Not long after the robin incident I was brought my first linnet; another cat victim. After a few days she'd recovered enough to be put in what I now called the Finch Cage with Chloe and Bully, as she was another little seed-eater. All three got on well together, and I was able to release Lindy Lou linnet five weeks later. She was left with a slightly droopy left wing but was anxious to go, banging against the cage door and twice escaping into the room and clinging to the window. She could fly, but not perfectly; I decided to take a chance. I released her in the garden and she flew into the thicket at the side of the Chalet. Later, I saw the linnet perching on a twig, preening. She seemed fine.

Sometimes one had to take a chance, the decision as to whether a certain bird patient could fly well enough for release being a difficult one on occasions, especially as I had no aviary in which a bird could fly across from perch to perch. Instead I had to go by how well they could fly across the small sitting-room without losing height. If one made the wrong decision one could be sending the bird to its death from one of the many predators outside.

One day I was called to a house the other side of the town where a lady said she had found a lost duckling. To make it feel at home she said she'd put it in her bath in a few inches of water. Could someone collect it? Arriving at the house I was shown into a pretty pale pink bathroom.

'There it is,' said the lady, pointing, and there it certainly was; standing in the pale pink bath in the water was a bewildered looking young pigeon.

'Oh, is it a pigeon? I thought it was a largish duckling,' she said.

Back home, the pigeon dry again, we had a good laugh . . .

Meanwhile Albert was pottering around quite happily outside. I hadn't yet put him in the duck-pen with Lucy; I wasn't sure how they'd get on and I wanted them to get used to seeing each other through the wire fence first. He took to following me everywhere – maybe the poor chap was afraid of getting lost or abandoned again – and he soon learned to climb the three steps up into the Chalet to look for me inside and potter around in there, too. Unless I shut the door. He was such a lovely fella that I forgave any little accidents and I used to put newspaper down here and there if he looked like staying in one place any length of time. If Eric was out, that is.

People calling with, or without, birds couldn't fathom Albert out. Some used to say, 'Oh what's happened to his wings?' a worried frown on their faces, or 'What, has he lost both wings in an accident?' looking even more worried. Children asked if he was a 'wingless goose' or 'Would his wings grow back?' Face-to-face with Albert for the first time as he stood on the patio, their confusion was understandable. I remember seeing Pam's brown Indian Runner duck in the distance for the first time and thinking something had happened to *her* wings! Yes, Albert's shape took a bit of getting used to.

On his third day outside I lifted the tall drake over the fence into the duck-pen with Lucy and stood and watched. They didn't appear particularly interested in each other at first, but when Albert moved a little nearer, Lucy threatened him, neck outstretched and hissed warningly. He took the hint and walked away, keeping his distance.

Within a week, however, Albert and Lucy became firm friends. They made an odd couple: Lucy, small and brown and 'duck-shaped', and Albert, tall, upright and snowy-white. But I was glad they'd got each other for company.

In the evening, Albert liked to sit with us for a while, lying at our feet like a friendly dog while we watched television and sometimes relaxing on my lap. If the fire was on, he liked warming himself by that, too. He was eating well now: Go Cat, raw meat of any kind and soaked bread-and-water (he didn't like Lucy's favourite – bread-and-milk). He loved ox heart, too, and I used to save him all the scraps I cut from the meat prepared for Wol and Katy, who wouldn't ever eat fat or gristle. But he never liked chick crumbs, which my first eight young mallards consumed in vast quantities.

During the night I used to hear little quacky, splashy, slurpy noises coming from Albert's box as he ate and drank – and talked to himself. Most birds, including Wol, were quiet during the night, with not so much as a peep until they were uncovered in the morning – but ducks always seem fidgety during the hours of darkness and quacky, splashy, slurpy noises were often heard from the duck inmates of my room. In fact I couldn't imagine sleeping in a room devoid of these familiar sounds; often awake myself, I found them vaguely comforting. If I got out of bed, as I sometimes did, I used to have a quiet chat with Wol or Albert – or both – before getting back in again. I think they enjoyed it.

So Lucy had at last got the companion I'd promised her a long time ago, if not a mate. Somehow we couldn't quite visualize them mating, though in the months to come you could tell this did cross Albert's mind from time to time. Who was it said, 'The impossible takes a little longer'?

7

The Friendly Moorhen
and a Surprise Visitor

*T*oo-Too was a moorhen chick and no more than a day old when she was brought to me one morning by a couple who ran a country pub some miles away.

'She was picked up by some friends of ours at the side of a pond,' this lady said. 'No sign of her mum or the rest of the family at all. She was shivering and crying.'

I warmed the little chick in my hands until she stopped shivering, then popped her in a warm nest of soft hay in a box with a warm hot-water bottle, placing the floppy but very soft Orlon hat I had over her for comfort. This hat had been used for many baby birds over the years but was the only one of its kind I possessed; I don't think you can get Orlon nowadays. Baby ducklings loved it, and always quietened and settled down well under the soft warmth. I fed the moorhen chick stiff Farex, at first, which she daintily took from the end of a spent match, but after three days she was eating Go Cat and raw minced steak as well. Her body at this stage was about the size of a small hen's egg, black and woolly, and she had long black legs and thin spidery toes – unlike a coot's lobed toes – and a red beak with a yellow tip.

Too-Too grew fast, and eight days later her legs seemed to have grown much longer and her feet larger than ever; even as a small chick the latter were outsize. But her body seemed to be about the same size still. I made the moorhen a sort of outdoor garden box with a pen leading off in which she could run up and down, placing it on the patio. She was beginning to peck up food, now, and I sprinkled soil in the run and a piece of turf for her to peck at. As we had no grass, of course, our side of the fence, when I had time I took Too-Too round on to the big lawn the other side to let her peck around, as she was gradually eating more and more greenstuff. I sat on a rug as she pottered around, and I discovered she had an absolute passion for daisy heads, eating every one in a wide radius around me. She quite liked dandelion heads, too, but wouldn't eat the leaves of either of these plants. She was a dear little bird and very tame and affectionate; when not eating, she would lie close to my cheek if I lay down flat for a snooze.

When she was older the little moorhen spent most of each day in the duck-pen with Lucy and Albert. They were both quite tolerant and more or less ignored her. Too-Too swam and bathed in the pond and walked around in the pen, pecking at this and that and thoroughly enjoying herself. She was unafraid of the ducks. Gradually she developed her grey feathers underneath, becoming fully fledged at about seven weeks old. Then, for the first time, she became restless and I knew the time had come for her release.

One afternoon I put her in a box, closed the flaps and carried her over to the lake in the woods across the field. I decided on this lake, rather than the private one, because I knew there were other moorhens there and there were also lots of rushes and reeds for them to hide in. Moorhens are by nature very timid birds and like somewhere to hide. I set off down the garden and through some barbed wire into the field, then walked diagonally across it towards the woods and lake, the latter being completely hidden by tall trees. Passing through a fairly narrow gap I then walked round the side of the woods into another field, following the perimeter until I was round the opposite side of the lake. There was a clearing here where the ponies in the field drank from the shallow water. There were yellow irises, reeds and rushes at the water's edge and one sometimes caught a fleeting glimpse of a moorhen streaking across the grass and back to the water as one approached.

Opening the box, I lifted Too-Too out. She'd been crying and unhappy during our walk and was no doubt thankful to escape into the cool water. I watched as she trod warily across some lily-pads, then suddenly scurried into the reeds and disappeared from view. I saw several other young moorhens about her age on the lake as well as adult birds so I knew she'd have company. It was an ideal place for them. I thought she'd be happy there.

I trudged back round the woods and across the big field home. But four hours later I decided to go back to the lake to make sure Too-Too was all right. Several moorhens darted into the reeds as I approached but I couldn't be certain if one of them was her; I thought one probably was. All seemed to be well, anyway; it was peaceful and lovely over there, and there'd be plenty of food. I came home again, feeling happy that I'd been able to rear her so successfully and had now returned her to her natural habitat.

The following afternoon, almost exactly twenty-four hours later, I was working in the kitchen when I thought I heard the cry of a moorhen outside. Funny, I thought, sounds just like Too-Too. I went on with what I was doing, thinking I was imagining things. But the cry came again. I opened the kitchen door and looked out . . . it *was* Too-Too! There she was standing outside on the patio at the bottom of the steps up to the door. Scarcely believing my own eyes, I watched as she stepped daintily into the kitchen and settled down for a nap in the bottom duck-cage, where she'd been sleeping these last few weeks.

To this day it's a mystery just how she managed to find her way back. I didn't believe her new flight feathers were developed enough for her to have flown all that way – moorhens aren't the world's greatest fliers at the best of times – so I presumed she must have walked. But all that way? There was the garden, a wide field, dense woods and a lake between us and where I'd left her, and I'd carried her there in a closed box. It was really extraordinary – I was truly amazed. And, equally puzzling, why had she *wanted* to return from what had seemed such a perfect place?

Anyway, here she was again. She seemed very tired but not particularly hungry and I left her undisturbed until morning. I had cleaned out her cage after taking her to the lake the previous day and put in new bedding, little knowing the cage would have the same occupant the following night.

Too-Too stayed with us another three weeks, resuming her routine as if she'd never been away. She swam and pottered round the duck-pen, stayed near me if I lay on the lawn, ate daisies, and was as sweet and charming as ever. Then, one evening, she jumped on to the coal-bunker, appearing very restless. It was 9.15 p.m., I remember, and getting dark; it was early August. I was inside doing something, but Eric, who was sitting outside, saw the moorhen suddenly take off and fly over the lilacs, disappearing from view. He hurried inside to tell me.

'Which direction did she go?' I asked, but he said he wasn't sure – it had happened so suddenly and unexpectedly.

'Perhaps she's gone to the river this time,' he said, as we stood staring across the garden in the fading light. 'Maybe she didn't like the lake.'

'Mmm, I don't know. How would she know where the river was?'

'They can *smell* it,' said my husband knowingly. 'They know it's just over there all right.' He pointed westwards – the river was only about three hundred yards away, as the crow flies, but there were tall buildings in between.

'Hmm,' said I doubtfully. 'Well I suppose that's it – we won't see her again now.'

But I was wrong. Seven months later in early March the following year Too-Too just as suddenly reappeared. This time she stayed around for two days, not wanting to sleep indoors but roosting at night somewhere outside, probably in some tree. Again it was almost as if she'd never been away; she resumed her old routine in the duck-pen and pottered in the garden. Then off she flew again. Five months later, August again, Too-Too turned up again, hanging around for four days, this time. She was less tame, now, but would come to me for tit-bits though she no longer liked being touched. After four days and nights she flew off again at dusk and we never saw her again.

But we like to think she's still around . . . somewhere.

And sometimes I lie in bed and think, 'I wonder *why* she didn't like that lovely lake?'

The usual early summer rush had been on: birds were usually brought to me in cardboard-boxes of various sizes, transported in various vehicles, but I was surprised one day when a lady knocked on the door and asked if I'd follow her out to the car-park where she had a bird in the car. It turned out to be a beautiful Rolls Royce and there perched on the pale grey upholstered back seat was a young starling.

'He started off in a box,' the lady said. 'But he jumped out. I think he prefers it on the seat.'

Starlings are nobody's fool.

Another less fortunate bird was a poor injured blackbird which was lying on its side in a yellow plastic dust-pan carried by a small child. I was horrified: the bird had been badly injured by a cat and it was lying there, uncovered and cold, like some dust that had just been swept up. I wasn't at all surprised when it died shortly afterwards. It is essential to keep an injured bird warm and preferably in a darkened box with some warm material or soft hay at the bottom.

One dark, stormy night a leather-clad motorcyclist arrived at the door. He'd come a long way in the pouring rain and, unzipping his jacket, he drew out a little sparrow. Happily it had been kept warm and dry that way, and it survived. Full marks to that chap!

Once I had two young starling fledglings brought to me. They'd been found in a loft and I called them Greengage and Blue Boy, putting harmless little blue and green PVC rings on their legs for identification purposes. I reared them in the usual way and then one warm, sunny day I carried their cardboard cage outside and placed it on the coal-bunker. Then I opened the cage door: it was time they practised their flying, I decided. They were feeding themselves nicely and could fly well – two necessary qualifications before release – and I was sure they'd be all right. They flew straight off across the patio and into the lilacs, then they perched on the fence, side by side, preening and sunning themselves and obviously enjoying their freedom. When they grew hungry, however, they sat there squawking at me for food, yellow mouths agape and wings fluttering, just like baby birds again. So of course I fetched the dish of bread-and-milk and obliged. Early evening I caught the starlings and brought them inside for the night.

This went on for some days. If I was slow in coming to feed them on the fence, Greengage and Blue Boy quickly learnt to fly through the kitchen window and find me indoors, noisily demanding to be fed. I started leaving the dish of much-loved bread-and-milk on a newspaper on the kitchen table – they knew perfectly well how to feed themselves – and eventually they got the message and were in and out all day long.

About two months after they first came to me as small fledglings, the young starlings stopped entering the kitchen. They'd grown up and gradually been coming less frequently, finding food outside. I often saw the two of them on the lawn, prodding for insects with some other starlings. I was pleased to see them doing so well, though I missed their visits; they were nice little chaps. Eventually they all flew off somewhere.

But I was in for a surprise one day: a very pleasant one. Exactly three years later, almost to the day, an adult starling with a blue ring on its leg suddenly started coming in and out of the kitchen window for food: Blue Boy! I could hardly believe it! Or perhaps it was Blue *Girl*, because the starling was taking beakfuls of bread-and-milk outside to feed three young starlings perched on the fence. This happened all day long and I was surprised and delighted to see my Blue again, especially after three long years. It was midsummer, too, and there was no shortage of food outside. Unfortunately, I failed to keep a record of how long this went on but I believe it was for quite a few days.

Greengage I also saw again, several times, but he or she never came into the kitchen again. He'd always been a little more cautious than the other one.

8

Owl Comings and Goings

'*W*ho was that?' Eric frowned, looking up from his crossword as I laid down the telephone.

'Oh, just a chap with a problem,' I replied vaguely, scribbling on a notepad.

'*What* problem?' asked my husband suspiciously. He suspected every time the phone rang it was someone wanting to bring round some large, noisy and awkward bird patient.

'Well, it's a peacock, actually. He–'

'A *peacock*? He's not bringing it here, I hope?' Eric interrupted, about to explode.

'No ... no, of course not ... calm down.' I explained. 'Apparently he's recently bought some peacocks and he says one has flown to the top of a tall Scots pine tree in a neighbour's garden and won't come down.'

'And I suppose he wants you to go there and get it down, does he?' Eric said indignantly.

'No, of course not,' I said again. 'He just wanted advice on what to do, how to get it down.'

'Hmmm.' Eric shook his newspaper irritably, far from satisfied I wasn't about to shin up a pine tree and break my neck. Who would get the supper?

I got some curious phone calls occasionally. Another panic-stricken chap wanted to know what to do about a gosling that was having difficulty getting out of its egg and another wondered if I could remove a large Muscovy duck that was standing in the middle of the busy main road and was disinclined to move; this at the dead of night. Eric's usual remark to a ringing telephone was, 'Tell them we don't want it,' before I'd even picked up the receiver.

Sometimes birds were brought to me under rather strange circumstances. For instance, one summer's evening a girl who worked at London Airport brought me a tiny black-and-white fledgling. She told me the little bird was taken from a passenger who was trying to smuggle it on board an aircraft but was stopped by the authorities. She said they'd been feeding it on corned-beef all day. It was a little wagtail, and sadly it died.

I had a tawny owl brought about the same time: quite a contrast. It arrived in a police car and the officer told me it was being attacked by two Siamese cats. It was a fledgling, probably a few weeks old, and was as adorable as Wol had been at that age, but this time I arranged for a very nice lady I knew to take him. She specialized in owls and had a special kind of rustic aviary on the edge of woods all round her large garden. From this owls could be released gradually into the wild, having been taught to fend for themselves. It was a slow and lengthy process and she'd been very successful over the years. There were owl nesting boxes in the trees; she and her husband were very keen on these beautiful birds. She called and collected my young tawny and I heard later he was reared and successfully released months later.

I'd been a little worried about Wol, meanwhile. He'd become unusually restless during the summer months and twice he'd silently slipped out of the slightly open sitting-room window without me even being aware of the fact. On both occasions I'd been busy indoors and had suddenly heard a great kerfuffle going on outside in the thicket at the side of the Chalet, with blackbirds and other garden birds shrieking their disapproval of some intruder. Hurrying outside I found Wol perching on a low branch and blinking in a bewildered way at the angry birds mobbing him. Garden birds hate owls.

'Come on, you silly old owl,' I chided him each time. 'What are you doing out here?' and I brought him indoors, where he appeared to soon settle down again.

But one never-to-be-forgotten evening he slipped out equally silently and unseen and we never saw our Wol again. It was my habit to put him in his cage for the night last thing before going to bed. He was invariably behind our two armchairs on the perch over the chest-of-drawers. On this occasion with the curtains closed and the usual bedtime jobs done, I turned to get him; no Wol. I looked around the room, puzzled.

'Have you seen Wol?' I asked Eric as he came out of the bedroom. 'He's not up there.' I indicated the perch.

'Isn't he in his cage?' Eric paused on his way to the kitchen, frowning.

'No. I can't see him anywhere.'

We looked everywhere, but no Wol. After a thorough search we decided he must have slipped out of the small top window again before we'd closed the curtains – it was the only possible answer.

It may seem very odd that neither of us had seen him go or even missed him in such a small room, but the fact is we hadn't. Wol's high perch was in the shadows and he passed the evening either snoozing up there or appearing to watch television with us. We simply hadn't seen his departure, taking it for granted he was still up there. It was very strange . . . and upsetting.

I went outside with a torch and searched the thicket, calling him, and all around the Chalet. No sign. Everything was dark and silent.

Next morning, I searched again. There were no garden birds making a noise and he obviously wasn't around. I was very worried about him – would he be able to look after himself? We'd heard owls hooting across the fields recently at night and now it seemed Wol had been listening to them too and had probably gone to find them.

That night I lay awake for a long time worrying about him. Wol had been with us for five years and he'd always seemed so content and happy . . . one of the family. In spite of his two brief sorties into the thicket this was totally unexpected. But now there was nothing I could do except hope . . . and pray . . . that he'd somehow manage and be all right. Perhaps the owls in the woods would 'show him the ropes' and he'd learn to hunt – a thing he'd never had to do? Or return to us if he were in trouble? We could only hope. We'd miss him terribly . . .

That autumn I had my first Little Owl patient. I was surprised just how 'little' he really was; although adult, *much* smaller than I'd expected. One of the nurses from the vet's brought him one Sunday evening, after someone had handed him in to them. There was no visible injury and she didn't seem to know where he'd been found or why he'd been picked up.

I put him in the lower part of the Finch Cage, Cucky Boy having now been moved to a larger cage on the chest-of-drawers, and offered the owl some pieces of ox heart. He declined this, at first, but ate quite a large amount of the raw meat during the night. He was with me four days, sleeping most of the day and fairly active at night; he woke me several times, being near my bed. He was eating well, too, and I couldn't really see anything wrong with him at all. Little Owls have a reputation for being very fierce but this one certainly wasn't – at least, not with me. Though his fierce-looking little yellow eyes were somewhat daunting, after Wol's dark ones.

The small owl took his departure at 3.30 a.m. on the fifth night. He'd woken me in no uncertain manner, rattling the front of his cage and clinging to the wire. Half-asleep, I crawled from my bed and quietly opened the front door. It was a cold, clear night but very dark; no moon. Reaching into the cage – with gloves on this occasion – I caught hold of the Little Owl and carried him to the open doorway, bleary-eyed and shivering in my dressing-gown. Without a sound he flew from my hands straight over the fence and disappeared into the darkness. I made my way back to bed, smiling as I snuggled down once more. He'd be fine.

'What was that noise in the night?' inquired Eric over his early morning cup of tea. I explained how I'd released the owl. 'Oh, I see – I thought I heard something. Any more tea?' he asked.

That winter Pam brought me another kestrel she'd had a few weeks. It was a young female with a badly dislocated wing and she thought it would be company for Katy, the one I had with two broken wings. I called the newcomer Claudia, and after a few settling in days on her own, put her in the cage with Katy.

Katy didn't like Claudia very much and screamed in the rather ear-splitting way female kestrels have of showing their disapproval whenever the latter moved. It wasn't a great success. Eventually both kestrels were taken by a very nice young chap I knew who kept birds of prey and had large aviaries. He hoped to breed from them and they'd have more room there. He already had a young male kestrel. It was sad about their wings but nothing could be done about this. Birds adapt wonderfully to their disabilities and to say, as some people do, that 'they should be put down' to my mind shows a lack of understanding. A really unhappy bird will refuse to eat and make the careful observer understand in many ways that life holds no more for it. But a crippled bird is still very capable of enjoying life in captivity, given the right conditions, of course; and has every right, I think, to do so.

9

Crows

I was having a spot of bother now with Crusoe. The silly old crow had taken to leaping into the air off his favourite ivy-covered tree stump near the duck-pen. In the evening he led me a merry dance just when I was tired and in a hurry to get him in for the night; he'd spring into the undergrowth and flounder around in the thick brambles and nettles and fallen trees, sometimes deliberately hiding and ignoring my cries of, 'Crusoe! Where *are* you! Come here, you little devil!' I'd be stung and scratched all over before finally grabbing him. 'I'll *murder* you, you bad crow!' I'd threaten, but he obviously thought it all a great game and often repeated the performance the very next day. Crows are like that. Being unable to fly because of his wing injury he couldn't possibly be left outside all night, of course. There were too many predators around.

Eric used to say, 'Oh, leave him. If that's what he wants, let him bloody well stay out all night,' but of course I didn't.

As if all this wasn't bad enough Crusoe sometimes launched himself into space with a giant leap for crowkind in the other direction, landing in the duck-pond. Three times I fished him out: the first time I just happened to catch sight of his one good wing waving around as his struggling body and the other wing sank under the water and I dashed out with my heart in my mouth just in time to save him. If I hadn't happened to see him through the window he'd almost certainly have drowned. It was the same the other two times. Something obviously had to be done: he might not be so lucky a fourth time. But what? He so loved perching on that stump.

Pam solved the problem by giving me some green netting she had. I rigged up a sort of safety net, stretching the nylon netting diagonally across from the fence the other side of the pond to the tree stump. It was high enough not to endanger the ducks but it would take my crazy crow's weight should he make a fourth suicide attempt. I could relax again, I hoped.

One day some people arrived with a young crow they thought was a runt.

'He's been hanging around outside,' they said, 'being fed by his mum. But today we found him over on his side with one foot screwed up. He got all messy and kept falling over when he tried to stand.'

He was certainly 'all messy' and it took me some time to clean him up. Then I propped him up in a cardboard-box. I found a small wound near his tail which I cleaned and treated with an antibiotic powder, then clipped the long flight feathers of his badly drooping wing that was slightly injured; I could do nothing about his screwed-up foot. The trouble there was that the hind toe had come forward and was sticking upside down through the front toes; this sometimes happens with birds. I once had a song-thrush patient that was badly crippled in this way. Crows in particular often have trouble with their feet.

I called the new crow Corby. He was much the same size as Crusoe, who was also a runt and smaller than the average crow. Corby's foot righted itself after a while and his health improved generally. After a few weeks I was able to put him in the cage on the chest-of-drawers next to Crusoe. They became quite friendly, much to my surprise. I'd had slight misgivings putting him up there as old Crusoe had hated every other crow I'd introduced him to, refusing to have anything to do with them. But he rather liked Corby.

The two crows spent much of each day outside together, perching on Crusoe's favourite tree stump and fooling around generally. But after a few weeks of this Corby started leaping off into the undergrowth and playing me up, just as Crusoe did. I wasn't too pleased at having *two* crows leading me a merry dance in the undergrowth! One night I searched and searched but couldn't find Corby anywhere. He was out all night and I spent a sleepless night worrying about him. But he reappeared the following afternoon. He'd grown fine glossy feathers by now and could fly after a fashion but not perfectly.

One evening Corby disappeared and this time we never saw him again.

Crusoe didn't seem to miss him, but continued running amok among the flowers and surveying the world from his stump. But two days after Corby's disappearance he did a stupid thing: he sprang from my hands after I'd caught him to bring him indoors and somehow fell on his head on the concrete patio. He lay there motionless and, horrified, I picked him up and rushed indoors. I nursed him tenderly on my knee, nestled in an old coat, frightened he was dying. He didn't die but it became apparent he was badly concussed. When he seemed a little better I put him gently back in his cage. I had to prop him up, with hay and woollies, or he'd have fallen over; he was very dazed and wobbly and didn't look at all well.

Crusoe was about the same next morning but when I came in from the kitchen some time later I found to my dismay he'd fallen on to the floor and was lying upside down on the carpet, legs in the air.

'Oh, no!' I shrieked.

'What's up?' Eric hurried through the door, thinking something terrible had happened.

'Crusoe's fallen again,' I moaned.

The thing was Crusoe had always loathed being closed in his cage – the wired door always had to be left open except at night. I hadn't wanted to upset the crow further by closing him in, even after he was concussed. But after this second fall, I felt obliged to close the Twilweld door for his own safety – until he was fully recovered, anyway.

Fortunately, Crusoe was a tough old bird and two days after his accident he was eating well again, although very dopey still. I'd been coaxing him to eat with his favourite food, and he'd now put himself on a diet of raw egg yolk, mince and mealworms, refusing other things. I noticed he'd slightly hurt his already gammy leg and also one wing. But he improved slowly and after nine days was almost back to normal. It was a great relief. We'd had him seven years and were both terribly fond of the old crow. We didn't know how old he was, as he was an adult – and certainly not a young adult – when first brought to me.

One day a girl who kept cats and often came here with a variety of birds turned up with four fledgling crows. She said her children had found them fallen from a tall tree; apparently two had fallen out of the nest the previous evening and the second pair that morning. Could I look after them?

Four large crows? The mind boggled; one was usually more than enough and where would I put them? Weakly I said I would take the young crows – Eric was out at the time – and I put them in the very large cardboard cage over the Finch Cage. The girl went home.

Two of the young crows were smaller than the others and all were very timid and yelled blue murder each time I caught hold of one to feed it. They were all reluctant to gape, which meant I had to force open each very strong beak – no easy task – to feed each bird at regular intervals. As sometimes happened, I began to wonder just what I'd taken on. A few days later, however, two of the crows learnt to gape and accept the food offered, but the other two stubbornly refused to open their beaks and, what's more, spat out everything I gave them. All four tried to jump out every time I opened the door of their cage and they still shrieked their woolly black heads off whenever touched. I was getting really exasperated with their awkwardness.

In the end I had to ring up the girl who brought the crows and she agreed to come and collect the two largest and most difficult ones and take them to someone who had aviaries and lived some twenty miles away. It was a great relief! I didn't like to admit defeat, but –

I got on much better with the two remaining fledglings. They were eating nicely now and had at last lost their fear of me. After ten days I had them walking about outside for part of each day, and three weeks later they were flying in and out all day long. I called the crow twins Cissie and Elsie.

Crusoe had been quite interested in the young crows. His cage was opposite and he could not only see them in the cage but he also met them outside on the patio. Elsie was slightly tamer than Cissie and after a while I put her in with Crusoe one night, as they seemed so friendly. But after four nights together I moved her back into the other cage: Crusoe had gone off her. He didn't like her perching so close to him and they'd been squabbling. He made it clear he'd like Elsie removed.

Cissie, on the other hand, was now roosting outside at night and refused to be caught. During the day both youngsters yelled at frequent intervals for food, wherever they were, and I dashed around with a large bowl of Go Cat or bread-and-milk to oblige. But, very slowly, they both learnt to pick up food and feed themselves. As always, it was a great relief.

Crusoe may have become disenchanted with Elsie as a nocturnal room-mate but outdoors during the day he'd got rather fond of her twin, Cissie. Round the thicket side of the Chalet, near the box where I kept bales of hay and straw there was a kind of bower formed by part of a fallen tree and thick, tangled ivy. Under this I'd casually thrown an upturned wire pen sometimes used as a run for small ducklings during the summer; having no bottom they could peck at the grass or soil wherever it was placed. Crusoe had recently taken to going round there each morning and solemnly standing in the wire pen under the ivy for hours on end. For some extraordinary reason he now preferred doing this to perching on his old ivy stump. From time to time I looked round to see if he was all right. One afternoon I looked and there was Cissie perched beside him.

From then on they both perched round there every day; at least Crusoe did. Cissie, able to fly, sometimes perched on a low nearby branch or went a short way away to feed. But she was never far away and she spent most of the day with old Crusoe, the two crows perched side by side.

It was really rather touching; my old disabled crow and the new young crow, Cissie, solemnly sharing an ivy bower. The routine was as follows: I lifted Crusoe out on to the patio each morning and he hurried round the coal-bunker to the side of the Chalet. Cissie, who roosted at night in a nearby tree, a few feet into the thicket, flew down immediately and ran to meet him, wings outstretched and giving what I took to be a glad cry: it was like Cathy and Heathcliff all over again. Then they both jumped into the upturned wire pen and crouched there, close together. They shared everything and ate from the same bowl of food, occasionally pottering about and pecking at things. At dusk, I caught Crusoe and carried him indoors for the night; then, and only then, Cissie flew to the tree where she roosted in the thicket. She never ever left Crusoe until then.

This went on every single day for five months. Cissie seemed genuinely devoted to the old crow; now a healthy young adult, she could easily have flown away – but she never did. Elsie had gone off some months previously and was seldom seen.

Then, on one day that I'll never forget, Crusoe hurried round the side one morning to keep their rendezvous as usual – but no Cissie to greet him. He perched in the wire pen, waiting, but she never turned up.

I was worried; where could she be? No sign of her on the low branch nor in the trees in the thicket . . . nor anywhere on the patio. What had happened?

I found poor Cissie later: she was lying dead under the tree where she'd roosted each night. Because of some fallen branches and thick ivy undergrowth I hadn't spotted her earlier. There wasn't a mark on her – no sign of any injury at all, and we never really knew what had caused her sudden death. She'd been perfectly all right the evening before and we could only think perhaps she'd picked up some poison somewhere.

I wished so much I could have explained to Crusoe why Cissie hadn't appeared. I couldn't, of course, so I showed him her dead body, gently carrying her to the bower; not through any sense of morbidness, I hasten to add, but simply because I hoped he'd understand she hadn't just flown away and deserted him. Then I buried Cissie in the field.

But I like to think her spirit lived on and was still with Crusoe – in the old upturned wire pen under the ivy.

Crusoe was with us another three years. Two years after his first bad fall he fell or jumped out of his cage again and became concussed for the second time: he was very dazed and unable to stand for some time. He put himself on a rather strange diet, when he recovered, scorning all foods except hard-boiled yolk of egg, very stiff Farex mixture, cheese-and-onion crisps and mashed potato.

Two weeks after his fall he became even more wobbly as one of his hind toes came forward through the front toes of one foot. My friend, Jill, came and took me to the vet: Crusoe was given a steroid injection which they hoped would help. But the crow was suffering mostly from arthritis and old age, I was told: I estimated he must be between fifteen and twenty years old by then, and had been slowly deteriorating the past six months.

However, always a one for launching himself into space, the old chap still continued to jump from his cage on the chest-of-drawers periodically, usually landing now in a strategically placed armchair. I don't really know why he did it; he just always had leaped around a lot. Naturally though, this jumping around didn't improve his condition. I tried closing him in and even moving him to another cage, but he was too old a dog for changes: it made him very unhappy.

One day when he'd been with us over ten years, Crusoe jumped from his cage for the last time. I was in the kitchen. Eric, used to the old crow's antics, called unconcernedly, 'Crusoe's jumped out again,' and went on reading his paper. I hurried into the room: Crusoe was on his back on the floor, legs in the air, between the two armchairs. Gently I picked him up and held him on my knee, but he died almost instantly, his neck broken.

It was a great loss but I thought later perhaps he'd rather have died this way. He'd become so infirm that I'd been wrestling with my conscience as to whether perhaps I ought to have the poor fellow put to sleep. But I just couldn't bring myself to do it. And now, with that final leap, he'd ended his own life.

That night in bed a thought occurred to me. Crows are strange characters, in many ways, and considered to be intelligent; I have learned, over the years, that incomprehensible things sometimes go on in their heads. People, I know, will scoff at my thought, but it was this: had Crusoe *meant* to end it all? Had he somehow instinctively known that time was running out for him and had chosen to end it in this way? Why had he landed on the hard floor between the two armchairs – and not on the soft cushion of the chair directly under his cage, as he'd usually done before?

I fell asleep pondering on this . . .

10

Two Special Blackbirds

Many young blackbird fledgings were brought to me in the spring and, a few days after the rescue of several youngsters, a girl came round one evening with an adult male blackbird a cat had badly mauled. He was in a bad way: part of one wing missing, all his tail pulled out and his back featherless, raw and bleeding. And very shocked, of course. I didn't give much for his chance of survival at all.

'I'll do what I can,' I told her. 'But I'm not too hopeful.'

I treated his wounds and then made him as comfortable as possible in a largish box in the bathroom. I put in food and water and a low perch; also the stone hot-water bottle wrapped in a woolly, as it's important to keep a bird suffering from shock very warm. Then I left him to it, convinced the blackbird would die in the night. Very few birds survived such bad injuries and shock.

But I hadn't reckoned on Bill Buster's fighting spirit. Next morning I looked in the box, fully expecting to find the poor chap dead. Instead, there he was standing on the perch, chook-chooking at me and with all his food eaten – where was breakfast? I was amazed and delighted, but I still thought a relapse might be on the cards. It never paid to be too optimistic with birds. They could be full of beans one minute and then suddenly keel over, often with delayed shock. I'd learnt to take nothing for granted.

I left him alone most of the day, keeping the bottle warm and just making sure he had more food and water. The following morning I crept into the bathroom, drew the curtains and gently removed the cover from the blackbird's cage, almost afraid to look in the box again. But I needn't have worried; Bill Buster – the name somehow suited him – was eagerly awaiting his breakfast again. *He* wasn't going to die – not him. I realized then that he was a fighter. Like people, some birds succumb to injuries and die while others fight to recover and do so.

Bill Buster lived and slowly recovered and grew strong. His back healed and he eventually grew new feathers on it and a new tail, but this took many months. He'd never fly again, though, as part of his wing had been chewed off by the cat and he only had a stump that side. After three months I moved him to the large cardboard cage over the finches, fitted out with twiggy perches, soil and clumps of turf. Later, I moved him to the large cage over Albert's; this I'd now linked to what used to be the kestrel cage opposite my bed by cutting a 'window' between the two. This was about seven inches square and gave the blackbird and any other birds in there much more room, obviously. It also meant I could slide a piece of cardboard across the window and make two cages again, or shoo the occupants into one cage in order to clean the other. But mostly they had the run of the two linked cages.

Over the years Bill Buster had a variety of companions and lived, I firmly believe, a happy and contented life. One of his companions for a number of years was a mistle thrush called Miz.

She had come from Pam's aviary and was another cat victim with only a stump of wing one side; Pam had had her several years but was moving house and so brought Miz to me. Bill Buster and Miz became firm friends and he used to sidle close along a perch and sing to her, very quietly. He seemed to prefer her company to that of any other blackbird I occasionally put in the linked cages; certainly he never liked any female blackbird I put in at all. They invariably had to be removed. But it was obvious when watching them closely that Bill was rather sweet on the big thrush. It was quite touching. When Miz died – of old age, I believed – Bill Buster was really upset and obviously mourned his companion of six years. But along came several other thrush patients and in time he quite liked these, too.

Nine years have passed since that poor injured blackbird was brought to me and Bill Buster is still very much alive and right here in the linked cages as I write. He sings beautifully at all times of the year, is tame and very friendly, and altogether a 'lovely fella'. I only once tried him outside in the six foot by two-and-a-half duckling pen I'd made (all Twilweld), but he hated it and was very scared. So I brought him indoors again.

Rambo was another interesting blackbird I had. Brought to me as a very small fledgling, he'd been taken from the mouth of a cat and he'd been blinded in one eye. This had become infected, together with his ear that side, and I took him to Steve who treated him with antibiotics. He recovered and grew in the normal way but because he was half-blind I was advised not to release him.

Rambo grew into a fine male blackbird and was eventually installed in the large cage over the finch cage: the one Bill Buster once had. It was fitted out with the same twiggy perches, soil floor, clumps of grass and so on, making it as natural as possible. I couldn't, of course, put him in with Bill Buster or they'd have fought tooth and nail.

I should mention here that across the room I had an Australian parakeet: a golden-mantled rosella I called Cookie. This seemed an apt name as he squawked 'Cook-eee, Cook-eee, Cook-eee' a great deal during the day. He also had a nice line in loud and piercing wolf-whistles, which greatly amused us; though he would never whistle if there was a stranger in the room.

When he was about a year old Rambo started singing: not just a dawn or evening solo but loud and long and on and off most of the day. He even sang when it was dark and he was covered up: early morning or late evening, summer or winter, it was apparently all the same to him. Now I'd had other blackbirds sing; this was nothing unusual. But Rambo had a claim to fame that probably *was*: I was sure he must be the only blackbird in the country that incorporated 'Cook-eee, Cook-eee' in his song together with loud wolf-whistles! Able to see and hear Cookie the parakeet across the room, he had learnt to imitate him perfectly, but with the clear, liquid tones of a blackbird and not the squeaky sounds of a parrot. So from then on one got a few bars of normal blackbird song, then a few loud wolf-whistles, further blackbird song, and then a few Cook-eee, Cook-eee, Cook-eees. It was most amusing.

Meanwhile, across the room in his big parrot cage, Cookie seemed to be struck dumb. It was some time before we heard him say anything again, apart from the usual squeaky noises these birds make. But months later he got his own back with a fair imitation of a blackbird's startled alarm call. This, so often heard when blackbirds are nesting in the area and they get panicky over something, was also occasionally heard indoors in our place when something upset or frightened Bill Buster – or some other blackbird patient. Cookie heard various other bird noises in the room on occasions and seemed to try to copy them. But he wasn't a patch on our Rambo.

Rambo is now over four years old and still singing away. In the spring I'm usually woken at dawn with one of his extra-loud wolf-whistles. It sounds funny in the still darkened room. Then off he goes, singing away like mad. But he always likes to start with the whistle . . .

— 11 —

Ducks and Drakes

A very sad thing happened one autumn. My brother was paying a rare visit and we had lots to talk about. Eric was out, and we were indoors having a real heart to heart. When we eventually went outside I was absolutely horrified at the sight that met my eyes: my dear little duck, Lucy, had drowned in the pond. I'd known the water level had fallen a little and had meant to top it up with the hose, as I usually did, but I'd seen Lucy get out of the pond all right that morning and, with my brother's arrival, had omitted to do so. Lucy, with her little twisted leg, had always found it more difficult to climb out than a normal bird would, of course, but she'd always managed. Until now. Now her sodden little body lay floating in the water with Albert standing nearby.

Quickly I fished her out but it was too late; Lucy was dead. I blamed myself terribly and wept on my brother's comforting shoulder. Then we went and buried the little duck in the ditch at the side of the garden, under some trees. How she must have struggled, I tortured myself thinking, only getting more and more waterlogged. If *only* I'd looked through the window and seen what was going on . . . if only? Poor Lucy, I felt I'd let her down. She'd been with me four years since being found injured and shivering, huddled against the wall of a block of flats near the river one cold winter's day.

Albert wasn't alone because he still had another young drake for company. He showed no sign of missing Lucy though they'd seemed very fond of each other. He'd always liked the other drake; in fact he seemed to get on well with most of the inmates of the duck-pen. He was an amenable sort of chap. He and Herby, the drake, were alone together for about three weeks, and then along came Daphne.

Daphne was a mallard drake and quite a character. The couple who brought him said they'd reared him from a baby duckling and he was very tame but they didn't want to keep him any longer because he didn't get on with their dog.

'We thought it was a female,' the lady said. 'That's why he's called Daphne. It's not only the dog,' she added, 'he's ruining the water-lilies in our pond.'

Looking at Daphne, now a handsome drake with a bottle-green head, I could well imagine the havoc he must have caused among the water-lilies. Knowing drakes, he'd probably been eating or nibbling them as well as splashing about amongst them.

The people also confided that they'd previously taken Daphne to Pam but he'd refused to settle so they fetched him back. I said I'd be glad to have him and they went away somewhat relieved, I think. I fixed Daphne up in the Lower Duck Cage in the kitchen.

Next day, I tried the new mallard drake in the duck-pen with Albert and Herbert. At first the former wasn't all that friendly, but they soon got used to each other. Indoors in the evening, I discovered Daphne rather liked human company, and he'd sit on my knee and enjoy being made a fuss of, making himself very much at home.

After about six weeks, however, I wondered if perhaps Daphne would like to go on the lake where I always took the other young ducks, so I took him there, cycling along with the drake in the 'carrier box' behind the saddle. Herby had discharged himself, presumably heading for the river, we believed, but I thought perhaps Daphne, being tame, would be happier on the beautiful lake where the owner would keep an eye on him and feed him.

But the mallard drake had other ideas: he was terrified at the very sight of all that expanse of water! He stood on the edge, shaking like a leaf, the very picture of abject misery, and no amount of coaxing would make him even get his feet wet.

'Go on, Daphne,' I said. 'It's lovely. Look at all those nice ducks out there!' But he wasn't having it – he just stood there shaking and looking very upset indeed. I brought him back home, where Albert greeted him with what I took to be a glad quack. Daphne went straight on the pond and swam around as if he *loved* water . . .

I sighed.

He grew very playful and loved pecking an empty yogurt carton around the kitchen floor, quacking with excitement and stabbing at it with his beak until it moved. I'd kick it back to him, and we'd play in this way until he grew tired of the game. Sometimes, in the winter, he'd lie at our feet like a dog while we watched television, enjoying the warmth from the fire.

We grew very fond of Daphne; he was now very much one of the family; as was Albert, of course.

About this time I had another duck arrive called Josephine. She was a large grey-and-white Muscovy duck and the couple who brought her had had her for two years as a pet, having found her covered in oil when a small duckling, they said.

'But we've just moved house and can't keep her any more,' they explained. 'We wondered if you'd have her?'

Eric wasn't around – he'd have had a fit! – so I weakly agreed. I could never resist a duck.

Josephine was about three times the size of any duck I'd had before, though, and after the couple had gone I began to have misgivings and wonder what I'd taken on. But she was a nice duck, very tame and friendly, and I hoped for the best.

'*That's* not staying?' said Eric when he came home, stopping in his tracks and staring aghast at Josephine, who was standing in the flower-bed eating a late chrysanthemum. I took encouragement from the fact that it was a question, not a statement.

'Well ... er ... yes ... for the time being,' I said slowly. I explained about the couple moving house. 'I'm sure they'll have her back if we can't cope, though. When they've settled in.' I spoke with more confidence than I felt; they hadn't exactly said this – it was more wishful thinking.

'Hmm,' grunted my husband going indoors. Then, minutes later, 'Where's she going to sleep?'

Good question, and one I'd been asking myself for some time.

'Well, er, she'll have to go there – at the foot of my bed.' I pointed to the big duck-box under the Finch Cage. Fortunately it was empty but I didn't want Josephine banging around in there keeping me awake at night. She'd only be a few feet away from where Albert slept; would they hold quacky conversations during the night or would she drum on the box with her beak? I hoped not. Anyway, it seemed the only place.

In the end the big Muscovy was reasonably quiet apart from some initial drumming on the cardboard sides. But Josephine made it quite clear from the start that as long as we were up she intended to be around too, and she much preferred sitting on my bed or in an armchair. Failing that, she liked to lie along the arm of a chair. Eric didn't mind her lying on the arm of his chair, he said, but one evening he complained, 'I wish she wouldn't *stare*, so. She does, you know . . . she *stares!*'

During the day Josephine liked pottering around our garden nibbling at things and sitting in the bird-bath, the latter being a cat-litter tray full of water near the fence. She liked to flop down in this for a quiet rest, now and then. She'd also come up the stone steps into the Chalet, wandering around like a dog. She was scared of Albert and Daphne and, when put in the duck-pen, jumped out again if either of them came near.

After nine days, however, it became increasingly obvious that keeping the duck permanently was going to present too many problems. She was just too large for our small place. She'd trampled on the plants; eaten most of my new wallflowers; and made an awful mess indoors unless I put paper everywhere. I had to admit, with Josephine, I'd bitten off more than I could chew.

I phoned her previous owner and they said they quite understood the problem. After a lot of discussion we arranged a temporary compromise: I'd have Josephine Monday to Friday and they'd have her weekends and holidays. They promised to have her back permanently, however, early in the New Year – if we could possibly hang on until then? They were going to make a new pen and buy her another Muscovy for company.

Josephine was my 220th bird that year. The total brought to me came to 223 by the end of December. I felt very tired; it had been a strain coping single-handed with so many under very difficult conditions.

The total number of bird patients was made up as follows:

39 Blackbirds	1 Lapwing
30 Sparrows	1 Skylark
22 Ducks	1 White pigeon
17 Starlings	2 Canaries
14 Blue-tits	2 Jackdaws
12 Song-thrushes	3 Budgies
11 Swifts	2 Goslings
8 Wood-pigeons	2 Greenfinches
6 Feral pigeons	2 Goldfinches
5 Mistle-thrushes	2 House-martins
5 Dunnocks	2 Little owls
5 Collared-doves	1 Magpie
5 Crows	1 Robin
4 Moorhens	1 Kingfisher
4 Coots	1 Black-headed gull
3 Great-tits	1 Racing pigeon
2 White doves	1 Great spotted woodpecker
1 Rook	1 Yellow wagtail
1 Cuckoo	1 Red-legged partridge

— 12 —

Pedro the Heron

*B*eyond what I called the thicket round the side of the Chalet there was a small field with ponies and two small stables. The thicket was really a piece of no man's land between our garden and the field. Between this small field and the big field often mentioned there was a wide ditch with trees and bushes each side and tangled undergrowth forming a kind of shady tunnel.

One morning I was hurrying back from one of my lightning visits to the shops when I found Eric talking to Shona, the girl who owned the ponies. She was telling him she'd seen a heron with a broken wing in the field, so I put down my shopping and went to try and catch him. Leaving Shona walking slowly up the side of the pony field, I went down the garden and through into the big field. Walking up that side of the wide ditch I soon spotted the heron, one wing drooping badly.

'He's coming through to your side!' I shouted as the bird crossed the ditch. I managed to struggle through the undergrowth and up the sloping side and through the dividing fence after him.

'There he is!'

Shona joined me and with widespread arms we managed to shoo the frightened heron into one of the empty stables and close the door. He was badly scared and stood dejectedly in the corner on some straw.

'He can stay in there if you like,' Shona said. 'I shan't be needing that stable.' She knew I really had no room for a large heron indoors. I was already wondering where on earth I'd put him.

'Oh, good, thanks,' I said.

She brought me a bucket of water for him and then, closing me in, stood watching for a few minutes before she left me to it.

Pedro, as I called him, had a broken wing and a small wound underneath it. I bathed this, clipped his long flight feathers that side and tied up the wing the best I could with some elastic bandage. The only fish I had was a tin of sardines, so I washed the oil off these and fed them to him, opening his long bill with some difficulty and popping them down his throat. It wasn't easy; he seemed to be all neck and long legs and kept struggling.

During the next few days I fed the heron tinned mackerel, some very large sardines and whitebait; he consumed the latter two fish in enormous quantities. I fed him by hand four times a day, trekking backwards and forwards across no man's land each time. This involved climbing over a low broken fence our side, walking the ten yards or so through the thicket, then squeezing through the wire fence into the pony field and crossing an expanse of mud to the stable. It was all rather exhausting; the weather was very hot and as well as feeding Pedro I crossed over many other times and back to make sure he was all right. I also left fish in his bucket of water, but, still very sorry for himself, he refused to pick it up.

Pedro had soon managed to get my elastic bandage off and I was still worried about his wing. One sunny afternoon the vet came with one of the nurses and they both clambered over to the stable with me to treat the heron; they were going to put a new bandage on his wing for me. I watched, somewhat alarmed, as they rolled the bird in so much tight elasticated bandage that he ended up looking like a mummy, both wings tightly bound to his body. I said nothing but I had my misgivings. One thing for sure, I mused – Pedro wouldn't get *this* bandage off.

I thanked them and the vet and nurse departed. It had been good of them to come. Eric's sister and brother-in-law were paying us a visit and I returned to where they were sitting out on the patio having tea and chatting. But indoors, pouring out tea, I couldn't help worrying about Pedro. I was also busy feeding numerous young fledglings I had; in between handing out sandwiches.

'For goodness sake sit down,' said Eric sternly, looking round. 'You're like a cat on hot bricks – sit down and relax.'

But I couldn't; twenty minutes later I once more tackled the mini assault course and went to see if the heron was all right. He wasn't. He was lying on his side, feebling struggling, his eyes closed. He appeared to be in a state of shock and unable to stand. I knew at once what was wrong and dashed back and into the kitchen for a pair of scissors.

'What's up . . . can I help?' asked my sister-in-law, Doris.

'Could you, do you think? Thanks.'

Doris got up and followed me over the fence and across to the stable. Pedro looked even worse and his breathing was bad; I thought he was dying.

'What do you want me to do?' Doris crouched beside me in the straw.

'Could you hold him while I cut this.'

As quickly as possible I cut away the elasticated special bandage that had been put on – there seemed to be yards and yards of the stuff. Doris was a great help; I don't think I could have managed without her.

'There – he's already breathing a bit better.' I stood up, the job completed.

Pedro recovered slowly and by evening was on his feet again. But it had been touch and go. That tight bandage had just been too much of a shock.

The next day the heron started eating again – he'd nervously regurgitated all his supper the night before – but something obviously had to be done about his damaged wing. Some days later I arranged for him to go to the Child Beale Trust's wildlife park some miles away and he was duly called for one evening and taken there. Later I heard that the poor chap had had to have the badly broken wing amputated – it couldn't be saved, their vet said – but it was a lovely place he'd gone to and I knew he'd be well cared for. There were other herons around, I understood, and many other species of bird in the park.

Pedro had been an interesting but somewhat expensive patient. And I was glad I didn't have to go backwards and forwards to that stable any more.

13

The Story of Emily

Emily was brought to me by three youths one evening in late spring. He turned out to be a drake but he was brown, like a mallard duck, when young, and I quite wrongly decided he was a female and so the name, Emily, stuck. The boys said they'd found him entangled in fishing-line in the river and that one of them had had to wade in to rescue the drake.

'He's got a bad eye,' one of them said. 'Think he's blind in it.'

I bathed and treated Emily's eye. It certainly looked bad but he didn't appear to be injured in any other way, fortunately. I put him in a large box in the kitchen – the duck-size cages were all occupied – and made him as comfortable as possible. It was five days before he'd pick up any food and during that time I had to get him on my knees several times a day and forcibly feed him. His eye was just a red blob still, in spite of antibiotics, and he'd been very shocked and unhappy after his experience on the river. I was pleased when he at last started feeding himself, usually in the night. On the eighth day I was able to move the drake to the large duck-cage near the bottom of my bed, under the Finch Cage, when a 'vacancy' occurred, and this gave him much more room.

Gradually Emily's eye healed but I was doubtful if he'd ever see out of it again. It had taken on a yellow, opaque appearance now. The second week after he came I was able to put him out in the duck-pen for a swim; I thought it would cheer him up. Albert and Daphne had to be content with pottering around the garden and patio, as I didn't want them to frighten the new boy. He was still rather timid. But the day after I tried all three in the duck-pen together and they seemed to get on all right. After this, Emily seemed well enough to be out there every day.

Five weeks later Emily was fully recovered and I decided to put him on the private lake where I took the coots and numerous ducklings. He was permanently blind in the injured eye but his other one was normal and he could see well enough. We watched him swim across the water under the willow trees and join a little posse of other ducks. Everything seemed all right. As I turned away I thought this was probably the last time I'd see Emily, unless he was still around next time I brought a duck to the lake.

The following spring I was delighted to learn that he was now a handsome drake – dark chocolate-coloured with a creamy-white shirt front – and that he'd paired with a young mallard duck and raised a family. I was very happy for him, and hoped they'd live 'happily ever after'.

But Fate hadn't finished with Emily; it was to deal him further knock-out blows. But for the moment we'll leave him swimming on the lake with his new family . . .

Later that year I had a very charming little sparrow brought to me by the RSPCA. A family had had the little bird for eight months, I was told, after she'd fallen down a chimney when a small fledgling, but now they needed a home for her as she was very tame and they were afraid of what might happen if they released her in the wild. So Daisy, as she was called, came to stay.

At first she was a bit of a problem as apparently she'd never been used to a cage nor eating from a dish. I was told she'd been allowed to fly and hop around the house and share the family's meals as they ate off the table – and sleep clinging to the curtains! This being so, the sparrow objected most strongly to the nice little box cage with all mod. cons I'd fitted out for her, preferring to be free in the room, and she eyed the little dishes of bread-and-milk and canary seed with grave suspicion. It was obvious it was going to take her some time to adapt. I let her flit around the room whenever I could, though, and she perched on our shoulders for a rest in between flying hither and thither. She was a very playful little bird and she particularly liked hopping around on the brick mantelpiece in the sitting-room. It had 'steps' up each side, leading to the centrepiece, where there was a clock, and Daisy liked to play with the various ornaments on each step. At bedtime she often hid behind the clock, not wishing to be caged for the night, squeaking indignantly when I grabbed her and put her in her cage. But gradually she got used to the routine.

She was a dear little bird and even Eric got quite fond of her. She amused us with various antics. On one occasion when I was about to do some sewing Daisy flew across the room and, with the flick of a beak, removed the length of cotton from the eye of the needle and flew off with it. She also pinched a skein of darning-wool from my sewing-box and a thimble mysteriously disappeared, never to be seen again. She liked resting on a convenient knee underneath the table when the owner of it was having a meal, but her favourite place was under my eiderdown; she loved snuggling under this. She was the friendliest sparrow I'd had since Chirpy, many years before.

Daisy grew slightly restless in the spring and I let her fly outside on warm sunny days and join the other sparrows in the lilacs. She was out for a while most days, but she flew through the open door now and then and played around indoors. She always seemed to know when it was lunchtime, and the second I put my plate on the table she'd appear from nowhere and position herself on my knee underneath the table, perching there quietly until I'd finished. Then she'd shoot off outside again. Gradually she spent more and more time outdoors, but she still slept inside at night. If I went out in the afternoon I always found the sparrow waiting for me on my return, and we'd enter the door together. Sometimes it was already dark, but she was always there, waiting nearby.

One evening, though, we had a shock; Daisy hadn't appeared. I heard the noise of a magpie and dashed outside to find it pecking something on the flower-bed, then it swooped away; was it our Daisy? But in the morning Daisy turned up again and it was a great relief.

But a month later she failed to turn up one evening and I never saw my little sparrow again. She hadn't been around to greet me when I returned from shopping, and this time we believed a magpie must have killed her. There were many around and she would not have been the first sparrow to have been taken. They were a real menace, and there were flocks of them in the field.

Poor Daisy. Yet she'd enjoyed her life to the full, and really had the best of both worlds while it lasted.

During the winter Cucky Boy had died. One morning I found him dead on the floor of his cage; he'd seemed quite normal the day before and I never understood why he died. It was a sad loss. He'd been with us two and a half years. The only other cuckoo I'd had was a very poorly looking fledgling that died within twenty-four hours.

Early in the New Year I got a phone call from the lady with the private lake.

'I think there's something wrong with Emily,' she said. 'I think he may have injured his wing or something. He's walking about on the lawn looking very distressed.'

It was agreed that they'd catch Emily and bring him round. He'd been eighteen months on the lake and had been fine – fully recovered after being blinded in that one eye. What could have happened, I wondered?

We lifted Emily out of the box and I examined him carefully. His wings were perfectly all right and I couldn't find anything wrong. I kept him indoors for the rest of the day, putting him in the Upper Duck Cage in the kitchen, above Daphne.

Next morning I put Emily in the duck-pen, and, watching him closely, I thought I realized what was wrong. He was stumbling around and bumping into things, acting very strangely and looking bewildered.

The vet I took him to confirmed my fears.

'He's got a cataract growing over his good eye,' he informed me. 'This often happens, I'm afraid. He can probably see light and shade, at the moment, but he'll eventually go blind in that eye too.' Wasn't there anything he could do? No, he was afraid not.

I brought the drake home, feeling very sad about it. Emily was young, still, and strong; the vet thought he'd adapt and still be able to enjoy life. So did I.

Back home, I put him back in the pen with Albert and Daphne. At first he continued to waddle around slowly, neck outstretched and bumping into things, and on the pond he'd often revolve in tight circles. But gradually, day by day, he got used to things and did, indeed, adapt. Within a month he was acting as if nothing were wrong. No longer was he revolving on the pond but was swimming normally, or quietly floating, and in the pen he walked around without bumping into anything.

'The fact that he could still see a little at first must have helped,' I said to Eric while we were watching him one day. 'He learnt to find his way around and knew where everything was before going totally blind.'

Albert and Daphne behaved very well and didn't bother Emily. I was afraid they might have done. It was almost as if they realized he couldn't see, I thought. I was satisfied we'd done the right thing in keeping him: Emily was as happy and content, I was certain, as was possible under the circumstances. I talked to him a lot and sometimes had him on my knee, but, unlike other drakes, he didn't really care to be cuddled much.

And so time went by and a variety of ducks and drakes joined the blind drake in the duck-pen from time to time. People seeing him had no idea Emily was blind until I pointed it out. Then, when he'd been in there four years, a dreadful thing happened one day: poor Emily was killed by a St Bernard dog, of all things.

The St Bernard, a beautiful dog that appeared to be well kept and in perfect condition, had wandered round here once before, years ago. I'd looked out of the kitchen window and seen this enormous dog standing in the duck-pen, his head filling the entrance of the little duck-house. Presumably he was sniffing at Albert, as I

discovered afterwards the latter was lying at the back, out of reach. I
shooed the dog away and even saw he got home safely: I knew he
lived quite near and that it involved crossing the dangerous main
road and I was worried about so lovely and valuable a dog getting
run over. It never occurred to me for one moment that he'd meant to
harm the ducks: everyone knew how gentle St Bernard dogs were,
didn't they? No: I thought he was just curious and paying us a
friendly visit.

But this time I was in bed with flu and hadn't seen the dog
approach. It was early afternoon and Eric said cheerio, shut the
front door and went off to catch his bus up the town. Next minute,
however, I heard his key in the door and he was back again, his face
grim.

'I think you'd better put your dressing-gown on and come
outside,' he said. 'That St Bernard dog's round the corner and he's
killed one of the birds or something.'

I slid out of bed and hurried outside, following him through the
gate and on to the gravel path that led to the car-park. What I saw
then I think will haunt me for ever . .

The dog was standing on the path at the side of the front lawn
over the limp, dead body of poor Emily. Chewing at him. There
were unmistakable bits of the drake on the path and on the grass: it
was grisly and horrible.

'He's trying to *eat* him!' exclaimed Eric in horror. And so it
seemed. Seeing us, the dog picked up the drake's body and loped off
diagonally across the tarmac car-park, heading for home.

I stood transfixed, not believing what I'd just seen. This was a
gentle, well fed St Bernard, not a hungry wild animal . . .?

I turned away and walked back to the duck-pen. The ground was
soft with recent rain and one could clearly see the large paw marks
and a few feathers that told the whole sorry story: the dog had
walked across the flower-bed and half flattened the low wire fence as
he'd walked over it into the duck-pen. By further paw marks and
scuffling, it looked as if Emily had been trying to escape into the
duck-house but had been caught and killed near the entrance. Being
blind, he'd obviously been at a dreadful disadvantage and hadn't
quite made it to safety . . .

We complained to the police and the dog's owners: I was both
angry and very upset. It seemed that the St Bernard spent a good
deal of each day alone in the garden of the house, with another dog,
while his owners were at work. It appeared that he'd taken to
wandering – and now killing – out of sheer boredom.

It took me a long time to get over the horror of it all . . .

14

Edward Woody and a
Coot in Distress

*E*dward was a large, fat, lumpy wood-pigeon baby who had been found by someone's dog while out for a country walk. I examined him but he appeared unhurt. He was two-thirds fledged with already large wings which he fluttered at me, squeaking for food as he stood on tip-toe in the box of hay I'd placed him in. But I didn't give him any – not then, because Edward's crop was like a hard tennis ball, crammed full of corn. So full-to-bursting was it that I became alarmed and wondered if his parents had overdone it and he'd die; he was too young to have fed himself.

'No food for you, my lad,' I told him. 'Well, perhaps a drop of Farex . . . later.'

He looked as if he might be able to get out of the open box, so I moved the young wood-pigeon into my largest hat-box with a lid. It wasn't quite like the four others I had, the square type with hinged lids that came from a store that sold millinery; this one I made myself, copying them but making it larger.

Next morning I was really surprised to find Edward's crop had deflated like a pricked balloon and was now empty. I fed him some Farex and then a mixture of stale brown bread and wheat, moistened with water into feedable lumps. In spite of being gorged the evening before Edward now reckoned he was starving and ate greedily. I fed him roughly every two hours, keeping him to the same food.

Ten days later he'd graduated to a bathroom cage – the only 'vacancy' I had – and after three weeks was mostly outside and able to fly. It was a month, however, before he reluctantly started feeding himself. Shortly after this, Edward disappeared. He was out all night and I'd been worried, but he reappeared next morning, standing on the coal-bunker and fluttering his wings at me and squeaking for food like a baby bird again.

For the next two months Edward kept coming and going. He took to landing suddenly on the ledge outside the kitchen window and then jumping into the kitchen for food. Usually he did this two or three times a day, at least. I developed the habit of 'talking' to the wood-pigeon in his own language. He'd stand on the ledge, peering into the kitchen, and make a sort of low, grunty noise; 'Mmmm, mmmm'. I would 'Mmmm, mmmm,' back at him; I learnt to imitate him almost exactly, with a little practice. We would keep this up for several minutes each time he arrived and I happened to be in there. I'm sure we had some most interesting conversations.

Eight months later Edward was still around, though he came to the window less frequently. We still had our 'chats' and he still allowed me to touch his back, shivering when I did so. He was very tame and friendly still; a full grown, handsome wood-pigeon now. Then for two months Edward stayed away, but we'd seen him pecking around on the lawn . . . with a mate.

'Look!' I called to Eric one day. 'There's Edward . . . with another 'woody'.

We saw them together quite a few times, after that. Edward was just over a year old, now; it was September again. Then one day he came to the window again, visiting us twice. Five days later, I saw him standing on Crusoe's favourite ivy-covered tree stump at the side of the duck-pen and he grunted at me when I walked towards him. I politely grunted back. His mate was usually around and we often saw her waiting in the pear-tree down the garden, but she never came near the Chalet.

Edward came to the window-ledge a few more times towards the end of October, then we didn't see him again. We thought perhaps his mate had got tired of hanging around while he paid us visits and had perhaps enticed him into the big field, where there were big flocks of wood-pigeons.

Edward was still a young fledgling when Eric and I were down by the river one Sunday afternoon. Suddenly I heard the distressed cries of a coot. They were coming from one of the islands in the river where there were weeping willows overhanging the water and quite dense undergrowth. I couldn't see anything – just hear the cries.

'Listen!' I said. 'It's a coot and it sounds as if it's caught up or something.' I stared across the wide expanse of river, feeling helpless as the cries continued.

'It'll be all right,' Eric said impatiently. 'Come on . . . I'm going home.'

'But it doesn't sound at all all right.' Why did he *always* say 'It'll be all right' when as often as not things were not all right at all? He stomped off and I followed him, slowly and reluctantly, over the bridge, still very worried about the coot. Back home, I knew I had to do something about it.

'I'm going back to the river,' I said curtly.

'You don't want to get involved.' Eric was putting the kettle on, more interested in a cup of tea. 'Forget about it.'

I strongly disapproved of this attitude. I felt that there'd be less cruelty to animals and children if more people who *could* help were a bit more courageous and *did* get involved. Eric's shoulder-shrugging 'none-of-our-business' attitude had always been a constant source of irritation. Now it was my turn to stomp off angrily.

I cycled back to the river. The cries were even more harrowing now, so, wheeling my bike, I went to a boathouse about fifty yards away. The man there was very understanding and agreed to help. Within minutes he'd stopped two people in a punt with an outboard motor and they drew alongside.

'Can you take this lady to rescue a bird?' the man asked, pointing up the river in the direction of the coot.

They looked a little surprised.

'Well, er, yes,' the chap in the punt said and his wife moved over while I clambered aboard the narrow boat. Soon we were chugging along and under one of the several arches of the bridge until we came to the island. Then it was difficult: I lay full length on my stomach, keeping my head low, as the punt was very slowly manoeuvred so that I was right under the low willow branches. With hands outstretched I still only just managed to lean over and grab the young coot – the one that was making all the noise. It was lying in a wet and dilapidated looking nest, half in the water. Its legs appeared to be paralysed and there was a dead mallard duck beside it. No sign of any other birds.

'Got it!' I cried triumphantly.

'Oh, good,' the couple in the punt chorused vaguely. They took me back to where I'd left my bike. Thanking them profusely, I put the coot in the large box permanently attached on the carrier behind the saddle and went home. I wondered about the dead mallard: what was it doing in a coot's nest? And why had it died? And what had happened to the young coot's legs? It all seemed rather strange.

'You've got it, then?' was Eric's only remark as he looked up from his paper.

'Yes.'

A few days later the coot was able to stand and seemed fully recovered. His legs were not injured in any way and I came to the conclusion that it was perhaps some traumatic experience that had temporarily made him lose the use of them. What had happened under those willow trees?

I put him in the duck-pen later with Albert and Daphne. Happily they all got on all right together. But after about ten days the coot decided it was time he moved on, and one day I found he was missing. I hadn't seen him go, so I searched around: no coot. Eventually I found him: he was on the footpath of the main road apparently *walking* back to the river; well, he was certainly heading that way. Catching him, I took him off to the lake across the field, where I'd first put Too-Too, the moorhen. He swam into the reeds and soon disappeared. He'd be all right there, I thought – safer than on the river.

I smiled to myself as I trudged back home; I was glad I'd been able to rescue him.

— 15 —

Patients with Hooky Beaks

Woolly was a baby tawny owl and he arrived one evening in the usual cardboard-box, having been found at the bottom of a tall, thin tree, I was told; the lady and her three sons who found him were out walking their dog at the time. Probably the owlet was just crouching there waiting to be fed by his mum, but the family thought he'd been deserted and so picked him up and brought him to me.

I put Woolly in the cage over Daphne in the kitchen. I estimated that he was about a month old with pretty mottled grey/brown/whitey feathers and a two-inch tail. He obligingly ate everything offered: raw mince, to start with, then ox heart or pieces of raw rabbit. I used to get him out on my knee to feed him and for a quick cuddle – baby owls are so incredibly cuddly and he seemed to enjoy it – and then he slept most of the day, waking up around tea-time and eating on and off during the evening.

In the evening Woolly liked to perch on the arm of one of our armchairs, watching all that was going on. He didn't like lights very much and when he was around I tried to turn off all except perhaps two lamps, so the glare didn't bother him. It was while he was perched on the arm of my chair one evening that he first became aware of Lulu. She was a very tame little one-eyed duck that I had at the time and she was in the habit of sitting on another chair (actually it was an old car seat covered with a rug and had no arms) near the television; almost opposite the armchair I was sitting in.

On this occasion the little mallard duck was relaxing on her car seat, head under wing, minding her own business, when Woolly suddenly saw her. He stared fixedly at the duck, head bobbing madly, his attention riveted on this un-owl-like creature; I don't suppose he'd ever seen a duck before. Lulu ignored him, her one eye

Lulu and Woolly.

peeping out from under her wing as it usually was: she could take owls or leave them.

Next evening Woolly, who'd been practising his flying round the room, alighted on the arm of my chair as usual. Then he suddenly fluttered across the three feet dividing the two chairs and perched beside Lulu. The latter stood up, glanced at the young owl and then calmly nibbled a piece of old Digestive biscuit that happened to be lying there, thoroughly uninterested in her visitor. Lulu *loved* Digestive biscuits. Woolly stood beside the duck for some time, mulling things over. The natives seemed quite friendly, so he decided to prolong his stay, moving a little closer.

After this the two shared the same chair for a while most evenings. They appeared to grow quite fond of one another, these two very different birds. My friend Vera's brother came over one evening and took some charming and very good photographs of the owl and the duck together (see p.xx).

Woolly grew fast and became more and more active. Ten days after his arrival he woke Eric up early in the morning; he was 'banging about' in his cage, I was informed, and Eric heard the noise through the wall, the head of his bed being against the wall dividing kitchen and bedroom. *Not* very popular. Two weeks later Woolly caught his first 'prey': an earwig. He pounced on it from the high perch over the chest-of-drawers (Wol's favourite perch) and made a big show of his catch: 'Look at me ... I've caught something!' holding the insect in his furry foot.

We felt he was progressing along the right lines.

Apart from sitting around with ducks, Woolly had the habit of stretching out on the table on his tummy, wings outstretched, 'sunbathing' under the table lamp. He also liked splashing about in his bath, a cat-litter tray, on the floor: unlike Wol, he needed no coaxing to have a bath and he bathed most days.

After he'd been with us three months Woolly the owl left us. He was a young adult now with beautiful plumage and I arranged for Alex, the young chap who had taken the two kestrels, Katy and Claudia, to fetch Woolly in order to prepare him for eventual release. He would be taught to catch prey and fend for himself and would gradually become less dependent on human beings: it was a lengthy process requiring time and patience.

Months later I heard that the tawny owl had been successfully released in a local forest.

It seemed quite strange to be owl-less once more; well, tawny owl-less, that is, because ten days later I had another baby owl brought to me: another Little Owl. He was a very small fledgling brought to me by Vera one evening: he'd been handed in to the local veterinary hospital by someone who must have found him; we never knew the full story. The owlet was about nine days old and so small he could just lie in the palm of my hand: a real mini-owl.

I made the little fellow comfortable in a cosy nest of hay in the top duck cage in the kitchen and fed him slivers of Woolly's left-over ox heart that was fortunately still in the fridge freezer compartment, quickly thawing out a piece. The baby owl made a little mewing noise each time, like a kitten, his yellow eyes staring out from the dark corner of the cage.

'He looks like ET,' remarked Eric, peering into the cage. 'Hello, ET!'

And so that's what we called him.

At first he was very scared of us and burrowed underneath his bedding like a mouse when either of us approached. But gradually the little owl became quite tame and was soon perching on a small log strategically placed in the cage. He always ate with great gusto, sometimes enjoying raw rabbit or chicken for a change.

After ET had been with us about three weeks I noticed his right leg, or foot, seemed to hurt him, and he took to holding it up and standing always on one leg. The vet came and said he thought the joint of the little owl's leg was damaged in some way; possibly it might have occurred if he'd fallen from his nest. Or he may have been hatched with this defect. The vet recommended bonemeal in his diet and this I introduced.

Over the next few weeks the owlet's leg certainly improved, and at about six or seven weeks old ET was fully fledged and flying well, practising the latter art round the kitchen. Like Wol when young, he enjoyed perching on our heads and would remain there until gently brushed off: he particularly liked standing on my head while I was washing-up or doing other chores. Eric wasn't terribly keen on having an owl on his head while trying to shave and I can well imagine it was somewhat distracting. But he was fond of our little ET all the same. The owl also enjoyed playing with various toys such as a large black rubbery spider and a pink woolly mouse; the latter he'd often hold by its pink crocheted tail and stand there apparently lost in thought for several minutes before dropping it. He seemed to deliberately drop the spider or mouse on to the kitchen floor in order to pounce down on them, no doubt all part of training for the real thing when the prey would be live.

One autumn day ET discharged himself by unexpectedly flying through the kitchen door when it wasn't quite closed. He landed on the fence and then flew off into the thicket at the side of the lawn. Later I saw him again near the lilacs, but he became scared when I approached and flew off into the field. I knew there were other Little Owls around because I'd heard them, so I knew he wouldn't be alone and I hoped they'd show him the ropes and he'd be all right. Little Owls are altogether more sensible than tawny owls, as a rule, and I believed he'd be able to fend for himself. They are partly diurnal, of course, and known to fly and hunt during the day as well as at night. However, I was a *bit* worried about him and so I took some lumps of ox heart and rabbit pieces into the field late evening and left them under the big sycamore tree where I'd last seen a little owl, just in case our small friend wanted them. I knew they wouldn't be wasted: some hungry creature would find and eat them, even if ET didn't.

As with all the birds that went, I missed our little owl. He'd been playful, gentle and quite charming during his stay, but the urge to be off had made him increasingly restless the last week or two. His leg seemed very much stronger and he was fully fit otherwise and flying perfectly: I was confident he'd make it.

I had two other birds of prey patients around this time: a kestrel and a sparrowhawk. The kestrel was tame, with jesses and a coppery ring on her leg: found on someone's garden fence, she was brought to me and then claimed two days later by her joyful owner. The sparrowhawk came two days later and wasn't so easy. I received a somewhat hysterical phone call from a lady living a few miles away to say there was a large bird crouching behind a bush in the corner of her garden. She thought it was an injured hawk.

'Could you manage to catch it and bring it here?' I asked hopefully.

'Certainly not!' was the emphatic reply. 'I'm much too frightened to touch it.'

'Well, er, have you got anyone else . . . a son, or neighbour, or friend who might help?' I was desperately busy and had no car or anything. And it was mid-evening and beginning to get dark.

'No, I haven't . . . I wouldn't *dream* of letting my son near it. It's injured and very fierce and might hurt him,' she replied indignantly.

I put the receiver down and sighed. I was indeed worried about the poor hawk. I rang my friend Alice and she agreed to fetch me and take me to the lady's house.

Together we managed to corner the frightened sparrowhawk, throwing an anorak over the bird and then putting it in a box. Back home I discovered it was a female and she had a broken wing. Badly shocked and scared, the hawk stood near the front of the cage I'd put her in with the one wing hanging down and the other one outstretched in a menacing attitude. She refused all food.

Next morning we took her to the vet who confirmed that the wing was badly fractured. A splint was put on and the sparrowhawk eventually recovered and started eating well, but she would never be able to be released. So Alex had her: he would breed from her and she'd be happy there with the other birds of prey in his aviary.

It was a good thing that excitable lady had seen her unwelcome visitor behind that bush, or the bird would almost certainly have died.

16

Podge

*P*odge was one of those pinky-coloured feral pigeons, who had apparently fallen from a building near a local supermarket. He was a large fledgling with wisps of gingery down still sticking to his head and neck and, though just beginning to pick up food, squeaked for me to feed him whenever he saw me, fluttering his wings. He was brought here by a girl who worked in one of the nearby offices.

I left him in the largish box with hay that he came in, popping lumps of corn and a squeezed out bread-and-milk mixture down his throat at intervals. I left pots of food and water in the box to encourage him to feed himself when I wasn't around.

After a few days I moved him to a cage in the kitchen. He progressed normally, and two weeks later was flying around outside. He expected me to feed him, however, whenever I was in sight and he liked to come indoors fairly frequently although I encouraged him to stay outside and peck around as much as possible. He still slept indoors at night, but after another few weeks, stayed outdoors less reluctantly, meeting other pigeons and leading a normal life.

The following spring – a year later – Podge was still around and as tame and friendly as ever. He always seemed very pally with any ducks I had, and often hung around the duck-pen. I noticed over the years that pigeons and ducks usually *do* get on very well together, for some reason. Podge had got himself a girlfriend now – a young, rather pretty black-and-white pigeon that I'd reared the previous autumn and released. We called her Poppy Peanut. As a fledgling she'd been found floundering in a river ten miles away and been hauled out: pigeons seem to make a habit of this, I could never figure out why. Did they think they *were* ducks?

Next thing I knew, both Podge and Poppy Peanut were coming

through the kitchen window regularly for corn, but after a few weeks of this, Poppy disappeared. Podge took to flying up to one of the smaller cages on top of the kitchen cabinet every day, where I'd put pots of food and water, and thereafter this became known as Podge's Cage. I put his name underneath, and from then on he came in and out several times every day and no other bird was allowed in there.

In between times, our friendly pigeon sunbathed on the fence, perched on the roof . . . or disappeared. We believed he was now roosting at night in some old derelict stables belonging to a hotel a couple of hundred yards away. Always he flew to and fro this same direction; across the garden and then turning in a wide arc towards his destination. I'd seen other pigeons around this building too. There were many feral pigeons around.

Podge came every day, never once missing, and this went on for several years. We got to know the times he'd appear and I worried if he was late.

'Podge in yet?' Eric would ask as he wandered into the kitchen. Sometimes I panicked.

'It's gone 12 o'clock and he's not in yet . . . you know he always comes at 11.30 . . . something must have happened!' I'd wail, staring out across the lawn.

'Calm down,' Eric would answer, 'he'll be here soon, you'll see. He's been late before.'

12.23 p.m. . . . and no Podge.

'Something *has* happened, I'm certain . . . he's never *this* late!' Outside on the patio I scanned the sky in the direction he should appear.

'Don't worry . . . you know he always turns up in the end,' said Eric, turning away and picking up a newspaper in the sitting-room.

At 12.40 p.m. there'd be a flutter of wings outside and up would jump Podge, attacking his pot of corn in the ever open cage with gusto, after cooing a greeting to me in the usual way. If I put my hand up to touch him he'd bow and coo and strut around in his typically friendly manner before continuing to eat.

'Podge! Where've you been?'

And so the days and weeks went by with the same routine.

Then, early one evening in August, Podge landed on the fence behind the duck-pen looking ill. One eye and his throat were swollen and I didn't like the look of him at all.

I caught him and bathed his eye. I wanted to keep him in for the night but he wouldn't have it; he was desperate to fly off again so I had to let him.

Exactly the same time the following evening Podge returned, fluttering down from the fence into the duck-pen. He looked much worse; he now looked very ill indeed and crouched huddled up against the wire fence.

Quickly I prepared the large rabbit-hutch I'd acquired that was round the side of the Chalet, underneath the bathroom window, putting thick newspaper, plenty of soft hay and two hot-water bottles in it. Then I carried poor sick Podge and gently placed him in the corner. I'd examined him first and saw his swollen eye was now closed and his throat was badly ulcerated, swollen and he was unable to close his beak properly. I put him on antibiotics and called the nearest vet, who came round early next morning. He thought it was 'thrush', a throat infection, but wasn't sure, and prescribed a course of treatment.

Two days later Podge was worse, huddled with his head in a corner, scarcely able to breathe. I was keeping him alive by feeding him three or four times a day with a mixture of very thin Farex and glucose, given with a small plastic syringe with a three-inch piece of valve rubber fixed to the nozzle. This latter I very gently and carefully manipulated down his throat, releasing a little of the liquid each time. His throat was rapidly closing and it became increasingly difficult, but it kept him ticking over. The stone hot-water bottle I kept hot round the clock, and he was well covered over each night.

Every time I handled the sick pigeon I scrubbed my hands with soap and then disinfectant and washed everything I'd used likewise. Throat infections of this kind are very contagious for other birds and I was afraid of spreading the disease.

I could see that another vet that came and saw him thought that there was little hope of saving Podge. He just didn't seem to be responding to treatment of any kind. Both Eric and I were convinced he was dying. On the morning of the fourth day he looked even worse; his whole head seemed swollen and his eye looked as if it would burst. His terribly swollen throat was hard to the touch and his breathing through the now tiny gap laboured: he looked dreadful and I was distressed to see him like that. I desperately wanted to save his life, but felt so helpless.

On Saturday afternoon I rang up Pam's son, Steve, at the veterinary hospital, in a desperate last-minute attempt to save the pigeon. I was sure he wouldn't last another day. Just on the point of going out – I only just caught him – Steve said, 'Have you tried Flagyl?' He added, 'It sounds to me like canker.'

'No,' I replied. He told me the correct dose and I put down the receiver.

Flagyl: where was I to get this in such a hurry? It was the weekend and I'd no car. Flagyl – the name rang a bell. I searched through a drawer where I kept medicines and yes, I had some! Little white tablets a dentist had once prescribed for me and I hadn't had to take them.

Feverishly I cut a tablet into quarters with a razor blade. Then I crushed one quarter into powder, dissolved it in a very little water and sucked it carefully into the syringe.

Hurrying outside I just managed to trickle the liquid down Podge's throat, taking great care not to waste any. Then all I could do was wait . . . and pray.

I looked in on him later, refilling the hot-water bottle. He was still crouched in a corner. It was a sorry sight. I wondered, as I covered him for the night, if this was the last time I'd see him; alive, that is.

Early next morning – I'd had a rotten night – I lifted the covers off the rabbit-hutch with trembling hands, fearful of what I'd find . . .

Podge was standing on the half-brick I'd originally put in the hutch as a perch; pigeons usually prefer this to a wooden perch. He was standing in a normal position and looking better; it was incredible . . . almost unbelievable! I ran inside to tell Eric.

Podge was still ill but some of the swelling had gone down in the night and he was obviously feeling a little better in himself. I gave him another quarter tablet of Flagyl in the same way, then continued during the day with three or four liquid feeds of Farex and glucose.

Next day the improvement had continued; he was really much better and even able to eat a little corn in the afternoon. His bad eye was now half open and he was moving about and looking out of the cage, fluttering a friendly wing at me when I spoke to him. It was almost miraculous – I couldn't get over it! I was thrilled; to think that a small piece of white tablet could have saved him from what we were certain was the brink of death?

After the seven-day course of the drug Podge's eye was back to normal and the ulcers gone from his throat, but I noticed that he had what appeared to be a large abscess inside his mouth, at the side, which was pushing the lower mandible of his beak to one side and keeping his mouth open, so he couldn't pick up food properly. So Alice very kindly drove me to the veterinary hospital and Steve quickly and neatly removed the growth. But the beak was permanently damaged at the side, through his illness, and it would always open crookedly, the upper and lower mandibles not meeting. Podge, I was told, should manage to pick up food and would adapt, but it would just be more difficult now. Rather like trying to pick up a pea with two crossed fingers, I mused on the way home.

I put the pigeon back in the rabbit-hutch once more, but three days later, completely recovered, he was raring to go and flew from the hutch at breakfast time the following morning. He was fine, flying around as if nothing had ever been the matter with him. He flew off, but reappeared at 3 p.m. and flew straight through the kitchen window and up into his old cage on the cabinet closely followed by his old flame, Poppy Peanut. Then off they both flew again, after a good feed of corn. Things were back to normal.

Eric wasn't too pleased about Poppy Peanut's return.

'I'm not having *two* pigeons up there,' he complained. 'One's bad enough.'

'Aaah . . . but they're so fond of each other – look!' I'd say, standing on the high stool to look into the cage and watch them feeding together.

'Doesn't matter – she can wait outside,' he replied firmly, glaring up at the cage. 'Out you go, Poppy!'

But when he wasn't around I'd shut them both in while they fed, and pretend only Podge was up there. You couldn't see without standing on the stool, and it would have taken a crane to get Eric up there.

Because of his twisted beak I made sure that Podge had corn and his favourite maples in deep dishes. These are a special type of hard, brown pea – much loved by homing pigeons. He definitely had difficulty in picking anything up from a shallow dish or the ground. I'd watched him in the garden and noticed only one grain of corn being swallowed to about every six he actually pecked at. But he *did* adapt and got much better at it, eventually.

The following winter Podge had one rather odd spell during which he stayed in for two nights, not wanting to go off to roost in the usual manner. Early one evening I even found him behind an armchair in the sitting-room – a thing he'd never done in his life before – but he didn't appear ill or hurt, I was thankful to find, so I just popped him into his cage and covered him for the night. There seemed no accounting for his insistence on staying in at night; it was very strange. I wondered if the old stables had been perhaps pulled down or collapsed, but, on investigating, found everything the same. So it couldn't have been that. But the third night he flew off as usual and it was back to the old routine again.

— 17 —

Jack and Friends

*O*ne fine sunny April day Jack came to stay. He was large and brown and still had a woolly appearance with baby down still attached to his developing feathers: you could just see a greeny hue under the fluff on his neck which meant he was a drake, all right. His previous owner hadn't been too sure. He was really a sort of unwanted baby, was Jack.

The girl who brought him explained: he'd been hand-reared from an egg by her neighbour, but it seemed the two other ducks this person owned disliked Jack intensely and they'd had to very inconveniently keep him separate at night. He just didn't get on with the two ducks at all and they felt they couldn't cope with him any longer. So Monica thought of me and it was arranged that Jack should come here. He was a Khaki Campbell drake.

So here he was, trembling and very nervous, sitting on my knee and being comforted.

I soon realized that the big woolly drake was a right 'mother's boy': a big softy, if ever there was one. He'd never known his own mum, poor chap, and those ducks had been really mean to him, he gave me to understand as I stroked and soothed him that first day. When I put him in the big cage at the bottom of my bed he just stood shivering and shaking and I had to get him out and make a fuss of him again until he relaxed.

Next morning I tried Jack in the duck-pen, where he met Albert and the others. Emily was still in there, at this time, and he hated Jack and pecked at him whenever he came near; Daphne was even worse and chased the big drake round and round the pen. The other two, Albert and Lulu, completely ignored him. It was *not* a success and I lifted poor frightened Jack out on to the patio, where he passed

Jack.

the day pottering around: that is, when he wasn't sitting on my knee.

Next day I tried again and this time the others in the duck-pen decided to leave him alone. Relieved, I went indoors, after watching for a while, but ten minutes later I glanced through the kitchen window and saw a kind of drama taking place on the little pond: Emily and Daphne appeared to be trying to mate with – or drown? – poor Jack, and, his feathers not yet being fully waterproof, he was floundering about two-thirds under the water and in great distress, the weight of the other two keeping him under.

I dashed outside and grabbed him: he was soaking wet and his feathers were saturated: you could have almost wrung him out! He was also very scared and trembling like a leaf again; indoors he took a lot of comforting.

I began to understand why he'd been brought to me: it looked as if Jack didn't get on well with *any* ducks or drakes.

After pottering around the patio and our small garden the rest of the day, and the following day, Jack tried the duck-pen once more. I sat outside and watched, this time, trying not to think about all the chores and jobs piling up indoors that I was neglecting. This time things did seem much better, however. Albert decided he quite liked Jack after all and later they even lay side by side in the entrance of the little duck-house. But Daphne was being very tiresome indeed, when in the pen, and seemed to hate Jack. Fortunately he, Daphne, now spent much of each day waddling round the garden – the main garden, beyond our fence – with Lulu. Daphne was rather sweet on Lulu, but it became obvious that the two drakes could not be left in the duck-pen together: if Daphne were in, Jack had to be out, and vice versa.

Anyway, Jack settled down and enjoyed himself pottering round our garden in between times. This was fine except for one thing: I discovered my new big drake was a compulsive plant-nibbler. Late spring he ate lupin and rose leaves, and early summer he specialized in newly planted annuals and any other succulent shoots. Mid-summer he ate or nibbled every flower in sight.

One day I went outside and stood aghast.

'Jack . . . how *could* you! Oh, *no*!'

He'd eaten a whole row of sweet peas I'd carefully planted out along the fence, leaving only bits of stalk here and there. I was extremely fond of sweet-peas and was really mad at him: 'You'll have to go back in the pen, you bad boy!'

The trailing lobelia in our two tubs didn't trail for long either; Jack found lobelia irresistible. Pansies – another of my favourites – were delicious, apparently, too. Sadly, all ducks seem to be compulsive plant-nibblers, not to mention crows, and Albert, being the tallest of the lot, was inclined to wreak havoc on most of the plants in the tubs, though I don't think he cared for geraniums.

Chrysanthemums were another plant I was particularly fond of: I usually planted out new young plants around early June. Now many of these were supposed to be 'stopped' or disbudded later in the year in order to produce good-sized flowers but Jack preferred to stop or disbud them a good deal earlier – such as, mid June. His method was hardly the approved one: he just ate the top few inches of the poor plant, along with any small tender leaves. When shooed away he pretended he was merely searching for worms and other insects in the soil near the plants: well, that's what I told an irate Eric one day.

'Well, why is the top of that plant missing, then?' he'd yell, rising from his chair and waving a newspaper at Jack. 'Get out of it, Jack! Go and walk on the lawn or something!'

Jack would waddle off, taking a passing swipe at a petunia as he went.

Jack moulted all his baby down and eventually turned into a sleek and handsome drake with the usual bottle-green neck. He seemed to get on all right with everyone now, and was even quite kind to the numerous ducklings I reared that year. Albert, too, always took a fatherly interest in the latter, even quite small ducklings, and was pleased when they graduated from the enclosed Twilweld duckling-pen to the open duck-pen, chaperoning them around in a kindly way. I think he was quite sorry when I gathered up the ducklings for the night and put them in a long cardboard pen I'd erected on an old radiogram Pam had given me. I think she intended me to use the radiogram for the purpose for which it was designed, but I found it made an excellent stand underneath our south-facing window for the duckling run; it could even be divided into two parts, if necessary, with a partition down the middle, enabling me to have baby ducklings down one end and perhaps slightly older ones down the other. It measured five feet long and was eighteen inches wide and fourteen inches deep. The two flaps covering the top were half cardboard, half Twilweld.

This pen was very useful indeed: I was pleased with myself for 'inventing' it! Sometimes we even played the radiogram underneath.

One never-to-be-forgotten morning the following year a fox killed poor Lulu. It had appeared some hours earlier and I quickly ran out and shooed it away, bringing Daphne and Lulu into our garden. But they were in the habit of walking round the lawn every morning, prodding in the grass for worms and other tit-bits, and so, confident the fox had run off – I looked but couldn't see any trace of him – I eventually let them out on to the lawn again. They'd been restless and fretting and desperate to get out. But this was the first fox we'd ever had round and I'd underestimated the animal's cunning: I believe now he hadn't gone away at all but was biding his time, hidden somewhere.

So Daphne and Lulu set out once more, working their way round the lawn. In the far corner they were temporarily hidden by a large bush. But only a panicky flustered Daphne appeared from behind the bush minutes later, and we never saw little one-eyed Lulu again.

Daphne was trembling and nervous when he fled back to the patio on his own, and I had to give him the 'comforting knee' treatment until he calmed down. After a spell indoors I put him back in the duck-pen with Albert and Emily.

It was very sad about Lulu and I was very worried, too, about the fox. Would he return? It was impossible to enclose the duck-pen and I like to give all the birds as much freedom as possible: the ducks loved wandering round the lawn.

Ten days later I noticed that Jack and Albert had become firm friends: in fact they hated being separated and appeared to 'chat' to each other a good deal. Then, nine days after this, Jack and Daphne became bosom pals, after months of the latter hating my big, soppy drake. No sign of the fox, thank goodness, so off they went round the lawn again, Daphne leading and Jack following everywhere the smaller mallard drake went: as thick as thieves! Albert didn't seem to mind: he didn't care for the lawn, shivering and shaking the only time I lifted him on to it. He was perfectly happy with Emily in the duck-pen, or pottering around our 'patch'.

The following Christmas Day the fox struck again, snatching

Daphne from the front lawn while he was walking there with Jack. They weren't supposed to go round that side but they sometimes did. Daphne was killed instantly and presumably taken away for the fox's Christmas dinner. It all happened in a flash and Jack came hurrying back to be consoled, trembling and nervous, just as Daphne had been when Lulu was taken.

And now I was even more worried. Apart from watching over the ducks as much as possible, there seemed little I could do about it.

Jack, of course, was very depressed at the loss of his walking companion and the fright he'd had. But later that year I heard of a brown duck that I thought might console him: she was on a farm and her days were numbered as the ducks there were bred for the table. I bought Winnie, as I called her, as a walking companion for the rather sad Jack, who had been duck-less for some time.

When they first met out on the patio Jack was scared stiff! Winnie, only slightly smaller than Jack, waddled up to him, and our intrepid drake promptly hurried away and hid behind the coal-bunker. Winnie followed, and Jack emerged the other side and scurried away across the patio. This happened several times and I was getting worried: could it be he preferred his mirror? Since Daphne's untimely departure, he'd taken to lying by a large mirror and gazing at himself most of the day.

It took Jack a week to get used to his new mate and then he stopped running and decided he liked her after all. And Winnie fancied him . . . a lot.

After that came the pantomime: Winnie kept flattening herself to the ground, outside on the patio, for Jack to mate with her, but my silly drake hadn't a clue what to do about it. He'd never had his very own duck before and no one had told him about the birds and the bees.

He knew he was supposed to do *something* . . . but how? There was Winnie, like a dart-shaped brown pancake on the concrete, patiently waiting: something was obviously expected, but how to set about it?

Jack stood at right-angles to the prone body and mulled it over. Then he stepped on her back, as if she were a bridge, and toppled over the other side. Winnie stood up; I could almost imagine her thinking, 'We've got a right one here.' She repeated the flattening operation, moving a few inches, and waited. Jack tried again, stepping on her back with one large webbed foot . . . and promptly fell on his beak the other side.

It was better than the telly! Watching from the kitchen window I didn't know when I'd laughed so much.

Winnie remained flattened and motionless. It had probably never been like this on the farm. Jack tried a third time, after walking round her once or twice, and got it wrong again: he was facing

Winnie's tail and, whoops! he'd fallen over again in a heap.

Eric joined me: he liked a good laugh.

Winnie, with admirable patience, shifted her position. But it was no good: Jack was hopeless. It was a good three days before he got it right, and then, after that, there was no stopping him.

Soon Winnie started laying an egg each day, sometimes in her cage and sometimes outside in the undergrowth. There was still a risk of foxes, of course, but I just had to keep my fingers crossed. At least Winnie would never end up on someone's dinner plate. And it was nice to see the now devoted Jack happy again, as they waddled side by side round the lawn.

Three months after Winnie came to stay, Albert, our much-loved Indian Runner drake, died. He'd been unwell for some time and in spite of visits to the vet, injections and drugs he became progressively worse and nothing more could be done for him. He was probably quite old – these ducks don't live nearly as long as mallards – and his breathing had become laboured: he had some lung infection. It was a terrible decision to have to make but I knew I couldn't let him suffer any more: the vet came, and it was all over very quickly. I buried him in the field and planted some daisies on his grave, watering them with my tears. It took a very long time to get over his death and I know Eric missed him too. Everyone who came here did: they'd all loved our tall, white drake. He'd been with us three and a half years.

— 18 —

Three Pheasants

*T*he spring that followed was one of the busiest ever: ducklings and other small casualties were coming in daily. Both ends of the duckling box on the radiogram were occupied, and by May there were five square hat-boxes lined up against the wall on my divan bed. Until I opened each one of the latter I wasn't even sure which contained which bird sometimes, so rushed was I. It was a question of, 'Let me see – I'd better feed these two little sparrows next,' as I flipped open the top of one box, pot of bread-and-milk at the ready, tweezers in the hand. Then, 'Oh, it's you, is it?' as a blackbird fledgling would be reaching up to me, beak gaping and small wings fluttering. Lid shut, then, 'Oh, you're the three baby greenfinches – I'll come back to you in a minute,' as I opened the next identical hat-box. 'Ah – there you are,' as I found the right box and ringing chirps and thin scraggy necks reached up to take morsels of the bread-and-milk. Most of the cages were full, too – there seemed to be birds everywhere.

The second week in May a lady arrived with three small fluffy pheasant chicks. She said the family had been strolling through their garden and these three chicks had somehow become separated and got left behind. Into another hat-box they went with the usual soft hay, woolly hat and my smallest baby's hot-water bottle. They were pretty little things, yellowy/fawn with dark brown stripes down their backs. They were only a day old and didn't want any food until the next day, when they ate tiny pieces of raw mince and chopped mealworm off the end of a cocktail stick. They loved this. I managed to make room for the pheasant triplets down one end of the box on the radiogram. There they had a warm bed and also some dry sandy soil to peck in; I scattered some seed and bits of food around on a square of turf I'd also placed in there, encouraging the chicks to feed themselves.

Soon they were indeed pecking about and eating things, but I continued to feed them individually every hour or two. On the third day I tried them outside on the lawn under a wire-pen to see if they'd peck at the grass and look for insects, but all three chicks just stood still in the sun and preened themselves.

A week after they arrived I installed the chicks in the rabbit-hutch outside, this time adapted with all 'mod. cons' suitable for young pheasants. They were growing fast and feeding themselves from dishes of chopped mealworm, tongue, chicken and any meat I had. At ten days old they were already partly fledged with leg and wing feathers and small flight feathers growing: game birds are able to fly when very young, unlike water-birds who develop their flight feathers last of all. The three pheasant chicks were flying well at two weeks old.

Most of the day they were out in the covered duckling-pen and only in the hutch at night. When they were about three and a half weeks old I had to move them into a bathroom cage for two nights as I needed the hutch for an owl (I began to wish I'd got *two* large hutches!). It was a tawny owl which had been found 'wet and ill-looking', I was told, underneath a tree early that morning. I made the owl warm and comfortable – out came pheasant bedding, in went owl ditto – put down food and left him to recover. He slept all day but as he hadn't touched the raw meat I'd left by next morning, I opened his mouth and popped some down his throat. I'd examined him but found nothing visibly wrong. I did, however, notice a rather hard lump in the owl's tum. I hoped this wasn't some growth. I fed him again late evening.

Next morning I was pleased to find the lump had disappeared. I decided it must have been food: had the owl eaten something particularly hard to digest and had this made him temporarily unwell, perhaps? He slept again all day but that evening became very restless and was fully alert, raring to go. Around 9 p.m., at dusk, I left the hutch door wide open so he could leave if he wanted to. Immediately he stood in the doorway looking out and bobbing his head; he was thinking about it. Half an hour later when I peeped round the corner he was still there, pondering. Then, minutes later, he spread his wings and flew silently across the garden and over the field, disappearing into the darkness. Another satisfied customer . . .

At six weeks old the young pheasants were fully fledged and the two cock birds had beautiful pheasant colouring and long tails growing. The little hen bird was browner, of course, and less colourful. I named them Phred, Phrancis and Phoebe. Phred was slightly darker than Phrancis, so I could easily tell them apart. They were very tame and I soon let them wander round our little garden. They loved the sun and spent a good deal of each day sunbathing, lying on their sides with their legs outstretched. It looked quite amusing to see three large pheasants lounging around on the flower-bed like this, but I'm afraid it did nothing to improve the nice show of flowers I'd hoped to have. One of them in particular liked to make a sort of cushion out of the poor Canterbury bell plants, the base leaves of which formed a round floret before the flower stems grew. Not many flower stems *did* grow, consequently. They tried to do the same thing with my favourite lupin, but this I drew the line at and put a circle of wire-netting round the plant.

When the pheasants weren't lying around in the sun they were often having vigorous dust-baths, literally smothering themselves in dry soil. This didn't help the flower growth either. There was quite a large plantless area of soil round the side, near the hutch, but it didn't get much sun and the pheasants preferred the flower-bed.

In between times they were stalking about on the patio and often came up the three steps into the kitchen. They were extremely inquisitive and liked to see what was going on everywhere, and they also liked to cadge tit-bits: bits of meat, usually, which they'd take from our hands.

'I shouldn't look in there, if I were you,' I once remarked to Phrancis. I'd opened the oven door to take out a baking-tin and the young nosey-parker was peering inside, neck outstretched. 'Don't push your luck!'

Later in the day when the sun left the flower-bed the pheasants flew over the fence and stalked, single file, up the side of the lawn. Their immediate destination was the remains of an old bonfire halfway up – the dry, white ash made lovely dust-baths and, as they were well aware, that side of the garden caught the evening sun. Afterwards, they sometimes strolled further up the side of the lawn and poked around for insects and other things of interest. Or they returned to the patio after their dust-baths looking like three white ghosts until they shook and preened themselves; it wasn't advisable to stand down-wind from them on these occasions!

Occasionally the pheasants flew on to the Chalet roof and pottered around on the flat part, directly over my bed; or they jumped up on to the coal-bunker and peered through the window into the sitting-room. The honeysuckle which spread for a few feet in bushy growth along the top of the fence was another favourite place; all three pheasants lay on top of this for a quiet snooze-with-a-view around mid-morning. Sun-worshippers that they undoubtedly were, they knew the honeysuckle got the first of the sun in our north-facing garden. They looked rather comical crouching up there, their heads peering out of the twisting strands of foliage, their bodies half hidden.

'You look ridiculous!' I used to say to them.

'It's not doing the honeysuckle much good either,' Eric remarked thoughtfully.

One afternoon I was sitting on the loo in our small bathroom. It was a hot, sunny day and the little window was wide open. Suddenly the head and neck of a pheasant appeared: Phred was standing on the roof of the rabbit-hutch below the window peering in at me.

'Do you mind!' I said out loud, staring at him. Phred apparently didn't mind and the next minute a silvery-grey foot appeared on the sill and he stood there, his whole body framed in the window as he stared, yellow eyes blinking at me.

'Go away ... shoo!' I said firmly, and he turned – somewhat reluctantly – and jumped down out of sight. Was there no privacy anywhere?

At seven weeks old the pheasants started playing me up at dusk, not wishing to be caught and incarcerated in the hutch. But I felt they were not yet mature enough to roost outside. They led me quite a dance chasing round the garden early evening and I was often puffed and somewhat niggly before I rounded them up and had all three streaking back across the lawn ahead of me towards the Chalet. I was amused that they always walked or ran in single file and never flew if they could help it: pheasants don't.

A few weeks later, however, they all insisted on staying out all night. I simply couldn't get them to come in, and they finally scattered in the undergrowth and disappeared down the bottom of the garden, probably roosting somewhere in the field. This became the new pattern: out all night, then reappearing early morning in our little garden. They were self-sufficient now and, though they sometimes ate the food I put down for them, they mostly pecked around and obtained their own.

I was worried about them being out all night, though, and one morning it seemed my fears were justified: only Phred and Phrancis appeared and we never saw Phoebe again. It seemed obvious that something had got her in the night, probably a fox.

Gradually the two cock pheasants – fully grown now and very handsome – came less and less. We just hoped and prayed they were keeping out of trouble and it seemed they were, for they usually turned up every other day, for a while. Then I suddenly didn't see them for quite some time and I believed they'd finally left us, but early one evening I was doing some weeding out on the gravel path at the side of the Chalet when I was surprised to see our two 'boys' approaching – not from the fields but from across the car-park: the opposite direction. Surely they hadn't been down the main road?

'Hello Phred . . . Phrancis,' I said, straightening up and staring at them. 'Where've *you* been, then?'

The pheasants strolled nonchalantly round the corner and up our path to the patio, had dust-baths, and then hung around for an hour or two, accepting tit-bits we offered. Then they strolled off down the lawn. I watched as they turned to the right down a muddy path and into the big field. I followed, and saw them stalking up the side of the field near thick brambles and hedges, pecking around as they went.

We didn't see them again. But during the winter I heard pheasants calling, sometimes, over in that direction and across in the woods and I wondered if they were the ones I'd reared. There was no knowing. I kept my fingers crossed for their safety.

— 19 —

A Chicken called Bunty

One summer's evening I was outside dead-heading a few annuals when a small boy came through the gate clutching something in cupped hands.

'What have you got there?' I asked, straightening up and smiling.

'A chick,' he said, opening his hands and revealing a day-old fawny/yellow fluffy chick. He went on to explain that he'd found it on an island up the river. There was a bridge across to the pleasure gardens on this island, and they had aviaries there with budgies and other birds. 'It was being attacked by a guinea-fowl,' the small boy added. 'See? It's got a mark on its head.'

It seemed rather a strange story: what were a guinea-fowl and a baby chick of some other species doing wandering around? But, thanking the boy, I took the little chick indoors and fixed it up in the usual hat-box with the old woolly hat and warm hot-water bottle. I wasn't at all sure what sort of chick it was: it was too large to be a pheasant or a guinea-fowl. A bantam, perhaps? I'd seen bantams over on the island. After two days I made the little chick comfortable in the long duckling box on the radiogram – the ducklings had long since gone – and scattered dry soil and some turf for it to peck at. It was very tame and unafraid, and during the day I carried the chick outside and let it potter around on the patio and in the flower-bed, as long as I was out there and could keep an eye on it, that is. I called it Bunty.

As it grew larger it became apparent that we had an ordinary chicken. After a month, ginger and black coloured feathers began to appear and the little bird sported a small comb. We began to dream of lovely new-laid hen's eggs one day.

'It might be a cockerel, of course,' remarked Eric drily. 'That comb seems to be growing.' He peered closely at Bunty, frowning.

'Can't really tell yet – hen's have combs too, don't they?' I'd made up my mind it was a hen: I was really looking forward to those eggs. 'You're *not* going to be a cockerel, are you, Bunty?'

Bunty grew very cheeky. She was spending more and more time outside now, pottering around and occasionally pecking the plants (oh no – not another one) when no one was looking. I had an invalid black-headed gull wandering around on the patio too, and Bunty bossed Gully around as she did the ducks, diving at them and chasing them away. It was late summer now, and during the still sunny weather Eric used to put a garden chair in a corner of the flower-bed against the fence, near the covered duckling-pen. This was in order to face the sun: at this time of the year, facing north, the garden was mostly in shade. Bunty, a sun-lover second only to Eric in enthusiasm, used to jump into this sunny chair and lie on her side, legs stretched out and eyes closed in bliss, sunbathing. She was extremely indignant when Eric returned from wherever he'd been to reclaim his chair.

'Get off, Bunty!' he'd yell, and she'd squawk with annoyance as he pushed her off. But the second he went indoors again the young chicken jumped back in the chair, spreading herself out to toast the other side.

Not that Bunty believed in lying on the ground when Eric – or occasionally myself – occupied the chair. As soon as you were settled, up she'd jump and lie on your knee, shoulder or even your head; presumably she worked out which bit of one's anatomy was catching the most sun and was available at the time.

Bunty mainly liked to eat raw mince and bread-and-milk, but would eat kibbled corn if nothing else was forthcoming and also liked insects and other delicacies she picked up in the flower-bed. She loved mealworms, too.

Very occasionally, I would get out the sun-bed and lie down on this on the patio for a quick snooze. Bunty, never missing a trick, would quickly jump up and lie on my stomach; possibly the warmest, softest bit? The noise she made if I dared to brush her aside sounded suspiciously like swearing to me.

At six weeks old, our chicken was getting more independent now, and was sometimes difficult to catch when I wanted to bring her indoors for the night. Squawking and running away behind the plants, she could also fly and used to perch on the fence to avoid my clutching hands. Often very tired, I used to get mad with her. Outside most of the day, she was sleeping in one of the kitchen cages at night.

Then, when she was about eleven weeks old, it happened!

'Cock-a-doodle-doo!'

It rang out loud and clear from the kitchen at 7.30 a.m. one morning: Bunty was a cockerel! So much for the fresh eggs I'd been eagerly looking forward to.

I hurried into Eric's room with a cup of tea.

'Did you hear that? Bunty crowed!'

'I told you it was a cockerel,' Eric replied, heaving himself up into a sitting position. 'I heard him sort of practising a week ago – didn't I tell you? Funny sort of noise it was.'

Bunty crowed again . . . and again. I think he wanted to press home the point. I reckoned he was still learning, as some of the cock-a-doodles sounded a bit off-key.

Bunty pressed home the point further still when he started growing long curved tail feathers and longer, darker-coloured neck ones. His comb was still what I'd describe as 'hen size' – not yet large and floppy. By his colouring, our Bunty was fast becoming a rather handsome Rhode Island Red cockerel.

It was November and the garden definitely short of sun. Bunty's favourite place was now the back of my armchair; he perched up there early evening with the radiator behind nicely warming his bottom. While draped in this position, breast overhanging the front of the chair directly above my head, he liked to be fed tit-bits, such as pieces of scone, cake or anything else we were eating at the time. Later, one very reluctant cockerel was moved into his kitchen cage for the night.

One day, just before Christmas, Bunty flew over the fence and across the lawn into the garden next door; I had to creep through a gap in the privet hedge and hurriedly retrieve him. He was a fully grown rooster now and I was having a bit of trouble with him; he wouldn't stop crowing. He crowed on and off all day: indoors, in our garden, and now – worst of all – in the middle of the front car-park.

'That ruddy bird woke me again this morning,' Eric complained. 'Six o'clock he started!'

'I know.'

Bunty had woken me up, too. He'd probably woken the entire neighbourhood. It was all getting a bit much: something had to be done. His crowing was positively deafening, especially at close quarters.

After much thought – I was very fond of him – I decided to see if I could find him a new home on a farm. Surely someone with free-range hens would like a nice cockerel? They didn't. I spent several afternoons ringing round farms but it appeared they'd got all the cockerels they wanted: too many, in fact. It seemed hopeless.

Early in the New Year Alice drove me and Bunty down to the RSPCA centre in Surrey, and Bunty went to live in their special enclosure with some hens, ducks and a few other cockerels. I was rather upset it had come to this but it was for the best. We hoped he'd be happy there; I think he was pleased to see all those hens.

I had another little chicken once; it was at a time when Jack was short of walking companions, I remember, and very soon he was out there pottering on the lawn with this newcomer. It was brought to me by a lady who had found it in her garden and looked after it for a few days; now she was going on holiday and could I have it, please?

It was a small black mottled chicken and at night it slept in one of the kitchen cages. When it wasn't the other side of the fence with Jack – they didn't walk round the lawn but stayed quite near – it was usually pottering around our garden, pecking at this and that and having dust-baths in the middle of the flower-bed. Growing fast, the little chicken was rather pretty: black, with lots of white speckles on its breast and two white centre feathers on each wing. It also sported a funny sort of top-knot on its head and had greeny/black legs with pink toe-nails. I thought it must be a bantam, but I wasn't sure: it was certainly quite small.

One day I had to go to the vet with another bird so I took the little chicken with me to ask Steve's opinion.

'Hmm,' he said, in a reflective sort of way as if talking to himself. 'One of them.'

Now I wasn't at all sure what he meant but the name stuck: One Of Them . . . OOT. So it became known from then on as Ooty Chicken.

Ooty was very good at keeping the magpies at bay: he hated them. So did we, because they killed many garden birds in the spring as well as stealing their eggs and young. The chicken took to flying at them, squawking like mad and sounding positively ferocious in spite of his small size; we thought it rather brave of the little fellow. If it rained, Ooty got underneath my bike which was leaning against the Chalet wall: there was a corrugated polythene roof jutting out over a few feet of the patio. He hated getting wet.

Ooty was with us about five months before mysteriously disappearing one morning. We never knew what happened to him: there was no sign of any scuffle, no feathers anywhere, and we hadn't heard or seen any predators. Sadly, we never saw our little speckled chicken again.

━ *20* ━

Claud the Crow

*C*laud was a new young crow that had been brought to me by one of the veterinary nurses; they'd had him since he fell out of a nest when a small fledgling (crows always seemed to be tumbling out of nests). I was told they'd had him about six weeks.

'He's very tame,' she said. 'He perches on your hand. We got quite fond of him, actually, but we really haven't the room to keep him now he's grown larger.'

I put Claud in the big open cage near the sitting-room door that Albert had occupied at night; I fitted it out with an inch-wide flat type of perch, which crows seem to prefer, and the usual thick newspaper on the floor. Just one perch gave him plenty of room to jump around. He perched there trembling and rather scared at first, declining the hand offered him: it was a strange hand, not the one he was used to, I could imagine him thinking. But he soon got used to us and settled down.

Like most crows, Claud enjoyed playing with things such as pencils, key-rings and small objects. In typical crow fashion they'd usually end up in his water-pot. He loved almost any food you cared to pop into his beak, especially any kind of egg or cheese: same as old Crusoe. I had another crow called Charlie in a big cage on the chest-of-drawers, and I'd rather hoped he and young Claud might become friends. But they were completely uninterested in each other: crows are very 'stand-offish', I always found. With exceptions, of course, as in the case of the friendship of Crusoe and the devoted Cissie.

Very soon I was to discover a rather odd thing about Claud, namely that he absolutely hated it outside. I could never understand this. He grew into a fine, glossy-feathered healthy crow, able to fly perfectly, but he was never really happy unless indoors perching in

Claud.

his cage. In the spring I sometimes persuaded him to perch on Crusoe's old ivy-covered stump at the side of the duck-pen and he seemed to quite enjoy this, though he never looked really relaxed. I think he expected something to jump on him. But, whatever the time of year and the weather, he much preferred to be indoors.

If not actually in his cage – which was always open except at night – Claud liked to perch on the arm of my chair; and sometimes in the evening to have his head feathers ruffled. All crows love this – Crusoe did, of course – and he'd go into a kind of trance if one gently brushed the head feathers forward with a repeated rhythmic movement of the hand; his eyes would close and his head droop further and further until his beak almost touched the arm of the chair. If I stopped he'd go on staying in that position, hoping the hand would start its caressing motion again.

'It's finished now, Claud,' I'd say, and he'd open his eyes and raise his head. Seconds later, he'd move a few inches and gently pull my sleeve for the soothing hand to continue – he hoped. But although crows can be soppy like this one minute, they are just as likely to give you a sharp peck the next. Old Crusoe pecked me on and off for ten years. Crows are like that.

Although Claud disliked it I sometimes put him outside on the patio and firmly shut the door on him while I cleaned his cage in the mornings; it was much easier than trying to do it with him still inside. Besides, I was sure it was good for him to get some fresh air occasionally. But, just like Crusoe, he got into mischief if shut out for long, pulling up small plants, pecking at flowers and enjoying Crusoe's old trick of playing with the now somewhat battered pieces of wood which were supposed to border the flower-bed round the other side of the Chalet. I came to the conclusion he reasoned like this:

'Okay, so they've shut me out. I didn't want to come outside – I was perfectly happy indoors. But now I'm out here and the door's closed I'll jolly well amuse myself: let's see, I'll start with this pansy . . . I'll pull this petal off . . . then this . . . then another. Now the stalk . . . get a good grip with my beak and up she comes. What's this green shoot? I'll peck that a bit next . . . and this little plant. Next I'll remove these little sticks . . . feet braced for this one, now a good tug . . . that's it. I'll just go and put them in my water-bowl . . . there. Now I'll go round the other side and play with those bits of wood . . . good game, that. She'll come out and yell at me but I'll hide behind that laurel bush until she's gone away. What – *fly* about . . . *me*? Perch in a *tree*? Whatever for? No fear. Cold and windy up there, I dare say. Ah . . . did I hear her open the door? I'll dash round and get back in the room while she's gone round the corner and left it open . . . That's better . . . now for a quiet snooze on my perch after all that hard work re-arranging the garden. She might even give me a bit of cheese if I sit here looking smug and don't caw too loudly.'

One Saturday morning Claud was outside on the patio as usual while I cleaned his cage and various things happened which made me completely forget about him. Hours later, I suddenly remembered I hadn't let him in and went and opened the door. There was no sign of him anywhere! I searched all round the Chalet and called his name, but he appeared to have vanished.

The rest of the morning and all afternoon I searched: in the garden, fields, road – everywhere. But no sign. And no answering caw when I yelled his name. What could have happened?

'Aren't you going to have any lunch?' asked Eric. It was gone 2 o'clock and he was getting ready to go out; Eric preferred his main meal in the evening.

'I can't – not until I find Claud,' I shouted, somewhat hysterically, I fear. 'I *must* find him!'

'Fox has probably got him – or a cat,' said my husband, always good at cheering one up.

I continued searching the thicket and undergrowth again, calling his name all the time.

'Claud . . . CLAUD!! Where are you?' Then I'd stop and listen, hoping for an answering caw. Silence, except the twittering of other birds.

It was early evening and about an hour before dusk when I heard him. I was in the field at the side of the garden when I heard a crow cawing, and I knew it was Claud. It was coming from the direction of the Chalet. I hurried back, panting – I was getting too old for all this – and called again, not sure where exactly he was still.

'Where *are* you?'

An answering caw told me: he was about fifteen to twenty feet up in a slender elm tree; one of many growing close together and entwined with ivy in the thicket at the side of the Chalet. He was perching in a small fork, almost hidden by the leaves and ivy. And he looked scared stiff.

'Claud . . . come on down!' I shouted, stumbling around in the undergrowth trying to get a better view, but the crow remained motionless, staring unblinkingly in front of him as if turned into stone.

'Claudy . . . come on, you silly boy.' I tried a more coaxing voice, gently shaking the tree – or rather, attempting to; the entwined ivy didn't help and another tree was less than two feet away. It was very difficult to even see him from directly underneath.

Claud remained motionless. He looked to me in a state of shock, unaware even of my presence.

It was getting darker by the minute, especially in the thicket; how could I get him down? I remembered an old ladder down the bottom of the garden and so hurried off and managed to half carry half drag it – it was very heavy and cumbersome – until I got it near the tree. But it was no good: the tree was too slender and the ladder much too heavy – and broken, in places – for me to get it in position. I abandoned it, after several exhausting attempts to heave it against the tree.

I looked around for someone to help, but no one was around. Eric wasn't back yet. Then I found a very long tree branch and with great difficulty managed to lift this into a vertical position – it took all my remaining strength – and gently prod at the frightened crow, trying to dislodge him. But he still wouldn't move. In the end, it took some minutes of prodding, shaking and yelling to make Claud move – it was as if he were glued up there – but at last he lost his balance and gave a sort of fluttering jump and landed near the coal-bunker on the patio. I grabbed him and brought him indoors, heaving a sigh of relief.

Claud was very quiet all that evening and all the following day; not his normal self at all. He stood on his perch and scarcely moved, staring ahead glassy-eyed, trembling at first but later quietening. He refused all tit-bits and seemed to be in a trance-like state: I believed he was still suffering from shock. The day after, however, he appeared to be normal again. I was greatly relieved.

This was the only time Claud ever flew into a tree. We think he must have been badly scared by something – some really traumatic experience – to have flown up there. What it was we never knew. In the years that followed he sometimes flew a few feet from the ground and, keeping the same height, round to the other side of the Chalet, but this was all. He had a rather odd habit of flying like this round corners, without stopping, and once nearly flew into me in doing so; I had to quickly step to one side as he whizzed round the side of the Chalet to the front door at the height of about two feet.

Claud also found a new game to play outside: it was called 'Rolling the Bottle', I think. It involved rolling empty milk bottles from the step outside the door, where they were placed, on to the flower-bed. He only had to pull or push them over for the bottles to roll nicely down the very slightly sloping patio to the bed. Sometimes they merely squashed a plant or two, but it was more fun when they smashed and the splinters of glass made a lovely mess. But best of all was when he successfully dislodged a new full bottle of milk, as he did on occasions, and then you had a really lovely mess of smashed glass and a pint of milk streaming down the patio; this was *great* fun!

Needless to say, this new game made me pretty mad, especially when I had both broken glass and the milk to clear up – preferably before Eric appeared on the scene. I used to take a swipe at the naughty crow with my broom or a newspaper, but he was adept at skipping out of the way with surprising agility and disappearing round the other side – until he reckoned I'd calmed down, no doubt.

'That'll teach her to shut me outside . . .!'

Claud also played less harmful games, like catching small stones or bits of wood thrown to him from about two feet away: he was very good at this. But *not* if there was a stranger there and you wanted him to do this trick: stubborn as ever, he'd usually decline to oblige. He liked to rattle small stones placed in a plastic flower-pot, too, and he was also an avid collector of empty yoghurt cartons which he somehow neatly stacked, as often as not, one inside the other in his cage. He particularly liked the now sadly unobtainable (in this area, anyway) blackberry-and-apple ones, carefully eating every tiny drop that might have been left at the bottom of the carton before playing with it. It was the only flavour he was really interested in: strange, actually, because he didn't care for blackberries and only rarely accepted a piece of raw apple.

Crows come and crows go, but they're all great characters. Claud Crow is still with us – and the same as ever.

21

Gosling in the Garden

*W*hen the pheasants were only about two weeks old I had another youngster come to stay. It was a Canada goose gosling. He came from the vets, having been handed in when found with a piece of fishing-line protruding from his mouth. He was about two weeks old, the same as the pheasant chicks, yellowy/brown in colour and very 'woolly' and cuddly: it was love at first sight again.

I'd never had a gosling to rear before and I was delighted with him. But a little anxious.

'What about the fishing-line?' I asked the nurse who brought him. 'Did the vet find a hook or anything?'

I was told that the line had disappeared before the vet was able to examine him. She said they thought the gosling was 'all right, though', and I hoped she was right. He certainly looked healthy enough.

I unimaginatively called him 'Goosey' and put him in a largish box of hay. I usually used hay as bedding indoors if I possibly could as there was less dust; it was surprising what clouds of dust came from even nice clean-looking straw when it was taken from the nylon sack I kept it in to put in a cage or box. Out of doors one wouldn't notice anything. Next day I was able to put young Goosey in the top Duck Cage in the kitchen, which gave him more room. During the day he mostly pottered around outside on the flower-bed and patio, pecking here and there and appearing quite happy. I had fixed a fairly large mirror round the side where the rabbit-hutch was, propping it against the wire-netting which bordered the 'flower-less flower-bed': a stretch of soil about ten feet by three which was heavily shaded by the very prolific and dense shrubbery which grew up to ten feet tall beyond the wire. (I say 'shrubbery' because I have yet to find anyone who knows the name of the plant in question. Growing like a weed in the summer it forms a formidable hedge with its broad leaves and tall, hollow stems, preventing any light getting through.)

Goosey liked it round there, sun or no sun, and loved the mirror. The older he got the more time he spent round that side.

One day after he'd been with us about a week I decided to take him for a walk on the lawn, so he could peck at the grass and anything else he fancied. The lawn had a nice selection of daisies, buttercups, clover and so on. I made him a harness out of two loops of nylon stocking, knotted at the back, and a long nylon 'lead'; years ago, I'd made a similar harness for my white Beveren rabbit and it worked very well, the nylon loops being very soft but strong. Goosey didn't like this contraption at first, but, like the rabbit, very soon got used to it. And off we went.

I didn't exactly take the gosling for a walk: *he* took *me*. Pulling hard, he dragged me all over the lawn, hither and thither. He developed an absolute passion for buttercup heads – fortunately there were many – and clover leaves came a close second. He also ate a lot of grass but ignored daisies and dandelions, refusing to eat both the flowers and leaves of both of these. He seemed to thoroughly enjoy our sorties on the lawn and I tried to take him for a walk at least twice a day, sometimes more. Goosey was still too young, I felt, to be allowed loose on his own out there. Each night I gathered a large bunch of buttercup flowers for his supper and he fell upon these and devoured them as soon as he was brought in for the night. I picked them in the field always, not wishing to deplete the number on the lawn.

When I'd had the gosling about three weeks I allowed him on to the lawn with Jack and Grandpa for the first time.

Grandpa was an elderly drake who had been walking round the lawn with Jack for about six weeks, ever since the sad demise of his mate, Winnie. He was about Jack's size and the same colour and of course Jack was delighted to have a walking companion once more, even though Grandpa couldn't waddle very fast and needed frequent rests. The old drake had been brought to me soaking wet and bedraggled by a lady who said she'd come home from work one day and 'found him in the garden'. She thought he looked ill. I wondered at the time how exactly he got into the lady's garden as Grandpa could neither fly nor even walk when he was first brought here. It seemed rather odd: had he been dumped by some uncaring owner, or what? The poor chap was old and somewhat arthriticky and lame, and his breast dropped very low, almost touching the ground, giving him a peculiar stooping gait. I installed him in a kitchen cage and gave him the usual warming-up treatment. Next day I lifted the old chap out into the duck-pen for a while, where he preened, drank, and seemed quite calm and happy out there in the sunshine. But I noticed he scarcely moved.

Jack stayed outside the pen, at this stage, looking through the wire and very interested in this newcomer. I didn't allow him in the duck-pen because I didn't want Grandpa disturbed.

Grandpa liked corn to eat best, but to begin with would only eat if I lifted him on to my knee and coaxed him, gently pushing his beak in the bowl of corn. I talked soothingly to him all the while; he liked being made a fuss of.

After four days the old drake stood up for the first time while outside; he'd been getting a little better each day and I felt pleased with his progress. Twelve days later I let Jack in with him and watched to see what would happen. All was well, and in no time at all Jack had somehow talked old Grandpa into going for a walk. I thought it was probably good for the old chap to take a little exercise now, and smiled as he obediently followed Jack out of the gate and down the side of the lilacs on to the lawn. At first he waddled rather slowly, but soon he was positively spritely, though still limping slightly and resting a good deal.

So now there were three on the lawn: Jack, Grandpa and young Goosey. At first I stayed near to the gosling and if I walked away he followed me. If I went indoors for a while I usually found him lying down or standing close to the other two, but he'd leave them and join me again if I went back on to the lawn.

Goosey was as large as Jack now and quite tall. He looked rather 'moth-eaten' with patches of pale grey feathers growing on different parts of his body. His wings were developing, too, and much larger, but there was still a good deal of baby down on him. He was very tame and affectionate, stretching out his neck to me and still making little baby noises.

Right from the first Goosey absolutely loved Grandpa and lay close to him when they rested. But this made Jack very jealous: he'd had Grandpa to himself for some weeks and he didn't much care for the gosling at the best of times. There was definitely friction: Jack took sly little pecks at Goosey who then squeaked, ran away and stuck closer to Grandpa than ever, which of course annoyed Jack even more. I used to watch it all while outside gardening, or from the kitchen window inside.

Goosey was soon growing his large flight feathers and I was alarmed to see he had an 'aeroplane wing' one side: that is, the outer feathers turned out from his body almost at right angles instead of lying close to his body. His lower abdomen was now white with grey feathers on his tum and feathers were appearing through the down around his face, and dark feathers on his back. He'd been with me about five weeks. Then, to my further dismay, the other wing went the same.

Since Goosey became large he'd been sleeping at night in the big rabbit-hutch, and at dusk I'd shoo him round the side of the patio and lift him in. He was always the last bird to be put to bed, the ducks coming in earlier. But something had to be done about those wings or he'd never be able to fly properly.

A friend gave me a lift to see Steve at the veterinary hospital with Goosey, and he taped up the wings into their correct position. It was a job I found very difficult. After seventeen days I cut the wide, pink tape off the goose's wings and was delighted to find the flight feathers normal. It wasn't always a certain cure but in this case it had worked: one wing was normal and the other almost so. Goosey should be able to fly now, when the time came. He'd been very good about the tape, which must have been uncomfortable. But it hadn't deterred him from his daily walkabouts with the others in the least and he soon got used to it. Now it was nice to see him waddling around pink-tapeless again.

The ducks and Goosey ignored the pheasants and this was reciprocated. They didn't meet very often: the former three were usually indoors or in the duck-pen by the time the latter took their evening stroll. Goosey usually spent the last hour in the duck-pen alone after the others had been shut up; sometimes he'd take a bath on the pond, displacing about half the water because he was so large. Fortunately the pheasants were already roosting in the fields at night by the time Goosey needed to sleep in the hutch – when he grew too large for the kitchen – or there would have been problems. Thank goodness I'd already proved the much-used rabbit-hutch was *just* large enough for a goose!

Late August that year the fox struck again. It was 9 o'clock on a Sunday morning, I remember, and everything was very quiet: no one much around. This time I saw what happened as I idly glanced through the kitchen window at the ducks and Goosey nibbling grass about six feet from the fence, almost hidden by the honeysuckle. It was all over in a flash: I was only conscious of a quick scuffling noise and a flash of brown fox darting back into the thicket carrying the poor dead body of Grandpa. The scuffling was hidden by the honeysuckle and I hadn't seen the fox emerge from the undergrowth, but Grandpa would have been killed instantly as all three birds were completely taken by surprise. Jack and Goosey ran away across the lawn, and I fetched them both indoors for a while.

Poor Grandpa. It was very sad but at least his time with us had been a happy one and I felt he really *was* pretty old and might not have lived much longer. We hadn't seen the fox for over two years and I'd really hoped he'd gone for good. Birds had been on the lawn all the year, on and off, with no hint of trouble; we'd almost forgotten about him. Apart from Phoebe Pheasant's untimely disappearance, that is, which was rather suspicious.

And now Jack was alone with Goosey. They still didn't like each other very much. Goosey was a fully grown adult and very handsome with a black neck and the white chin band. He was as tame and friendly as ever and I'd been wondering what to do with him: should I put him on the river . . . or on a lake . . . or wait for him to fly away and choose for himself, probably finding other geese?

After much thought I decided to put him on a local gravel pit 'lake'. Susan's garden sloped down to this very large expanse of water and she threw bread for the many resident and visiting birds: swans, ducks, Canada geese and other water-fowl; and their offspring. Some of them became very tame and waddled out and took bread from her hand. Goosey had been found on the edge of this water when a baby gosling and he'd surely meet up with others of his kind there. Also, Susan would be able to keep an eye on him and feed him with her other customers.

It was all arranged. But then I received an urgent phone call from her: the lake was covered in green algae – the sort that was poisoning animals when they drank and was causing great concern in various parts of the country. It had virtually happened overnight. We weren't sure if it would harm geese but thought it best not to risk it.

Goosey stayed on therefore, practising his flying now by rushing up and down the length of the lawn flapping his wings and almost, but not quite, becoming airborne. He did this every day. I believed he would like to fly but was nervous of 'taking the plunge', as it were.

Early one day in October, however, he was startled by a large Alsatian dog which came bounding into the garden from the field. Goosey took off and flew into the air, gaining height as he flew over the field beyond the lawn; the dog had proved to be the incentive he needed.

I was confident he'd be all right. We expected he'd flown further up the river where there were flocks of these large geese both on the water and grazing in bordering fields. But ever since then when the geese have flown overhead I've looked up and wondered whether my dear Goosey was one of them.

22

Pigeon Saga

*T*his is really the story of four pigeons: Punch, Judy, Snowy and Gonzo. It happened like this . . .

One day in early May a rather pretty girl arrived with a box. Stepping over our little rustic gate – few people bothered to actually open it – she smiled at me.

'Hello – what have you got there?' I asked, looking up from where I was weeding. 'Not a *pigeon?*' I'd promised Eric I wouldn't take any more pigeons; we'd had endless trouble with them.

'Well, yes – I'm afraid so,' the girl replied. She put down the cardboard box and undid the flaps, drawing out a very dirty, bedraggled white pigeon. 'I found him in the road near a garage – there are lots of them there. They're all dirty and thin, like this one. I think he's hurt his wing – he can't seem to fly.'

I sighed. How could I refuse to take the poor thing?

'Okay. But I don't really take pigeons any more.' I explained about the trouble we'd had. They make a lot of mess, eat food put out for all the other birds, and sometimes do damage to buildings. They also invite all their friends and relations round. You really need a good sized aviary for pigeons.

I called him Punch and installed the pigeon in the vacant cage on top of the kitchen cabinet. His crop was empty and he was very hungry: he ate from the big bowl of corn I gave him for several minutes.

Punch had what appeared to be an old wing injury and couldn't fly. I fed him up, and after a week indoors tried him outside. He walked about on the patio but seemed slightly dazed and when anything frightened him he fell over on to his back and just lay there, legs in the air, until I came along and righted him. But he ate well,

107

bathed, and soon looked much cleaner and whiter.

Eighteen days after the arrival of Punch the pretty girl stepped over the gate again: same time, around mid-afternoon.

'Not another one?' I asked, jokingly, looking up. I was gardening again.

The girl smiled apologetically.

'I'm afraid so – I couldn't leave the poor thing. This one looks half-starved and can't fly either. It's from the same place.'

She handed over a reddy/brown and white pigeon, smaller than Punch. We got chatting and I showed her some of the birds. I asked her what her job was, slightly curious that she seemed to be free during the afternoons.

'I'm a plumber,' she said.

What a surprise! Slim and petite, she wasn't like any plumber *I'd* ever seen!

'Oh. I see.'

As she left I called out, 'You will try not to bring any more pigeons, won't you?'

She promised she'd try not to. Not too pleased about Punch – to put it mildly – Eric wasn't going to be exactly thrilled at the sight of this new one, either.

It was a lovely sunny afternoon and I put the new pigeon down on the patio and gave it a bowl of corn, which it ate greedily. It was very dirty, the same as Punch had been. And thin.

Within seconds Punch walked up and the two pigeons ate together, and from that moment onwards they became inseparable. I just had to call the newcomer Judy. As I watched them together I became convinced that they knew each other and had possibly even been mates in that garage vicinity five miles away.

That night I put them together in Punch's cage and a few days later moved them to a larger cage in the bathroom each night.

Punch and Judy were together all day in the garden from then on. Whenever Punch fell on to his back – as he still did – Judy stood by his side until help came. One day I saw her standing motionless on the edge of the patio, near the flower-bed, but I couldn't see Punch. I went indoors, but a few minutes later she was still there so I went to investigate. I found Punch lying on his back under the very large leaves of a tobacco plant. The leaves were shielding his body to such an extent that when I first looked I simply hadn't seen the poor chap. He might have been there a lot longer if it hadn't been for Judy.

Each night I caught Punch and carried him round into the bathroom. Judy, plump and healthy again and able to fly, went round the side of the Chalet and flew in at the window to join him in their cage, after which there was much excited cooing; they greeted each other as if they'd been apart for days instead of seconds. They really were a most devoted couple. Punch tried to mate with Judy on occasions, but the poor chap never managed it: he usually ended up falling on to his back.

In mid-August, three months after Punch was brought here, two workmen in a lorry arrived clutching another dirty white pigeon. It had been shot in the shoulder. Once again, how could I refuse to take the poor bird, I thought? But – oh dear – what would Eric say?

The new pigeon's wing was very swollen and the flight feathers that side hanging down. I bathed the wound and taped up the wing, putting Snowy, as I called him, in the other bathroom cage under Punch and Judy. He was a youngster and only just beginning to pick up the brown bread-and-milk I offered – he wouldn't eat corn so I fed him in between times, pushing squeezed-out morsels down his throat. He became very tame, soon taking it from my fingers. Two days after his arrival, Snowy was out walking on the patio with Punch and Judy. The latter had the use of the old rabbit-hutch daytime. I left one of the hutch doors open and the ramp in place and they often went and sat in there side by side on a flat perch I'd made. Now they were sometimes joined by young Snowy, who was allowed in there provided he kept his distance; he usually settled on a half-brick a foot or two away from the others.

A week after Snowy came I was able to take the tape off his injured wing. It was still somewhat swollen, however, so I taped the outer flight feathers of each wing together over his back – just the tips – which stopped the drooping injured one from dragging on the ground.

Now and again there were squabbles in the hutch: Punch didn't really like Snowy in there; only just about tolerating his presence on the brick. He preferred to be alone with his Judy. Snowy soon learnt to fly into the bathroom at night, as soon as I took the tape off his wing tips. He could fly surprising well, actually, considering his wing still drooped badly, but usually he was content to walk around the garden and didn't bother. I think he rather fancied Judy and tried to court her, as he grew older, but he had the faithful Punch to contend with and was quickly sent packing.

This, of course, was the summer of Goosey and the three pheasants; the patio was often a hive of activity. The months went by and the three pigeons led a happy, contented life – well fed and clean again, Punch and Snowy shining white and Judy plump and well cared for. Autumn came and the days shortened with less and less sun on the patio. Goosey had flown and the pheasants departed for pastures new: the pigeons had the patio to themselves. Then came a fateful evening in late November; an evening I try not to think about too often.

It was a Sunday, I remember, and, very tired, I'd slept too long while taking an afternoon nap on my bed. I awoke to find dusk had fallen and it was getting quite dark outside. I should have got the pigeons in before this; Punch would be waiting outside the door for me to carry him through to the bathroom and the window there needing opening for Snowy and Judy to fly through. Quickly I put on my shoes and hurried to the door, pulling it open.

Right in front of me on the patio was the fox! Less than three feet away he stared straight at me, then as I shouted something like, 'Go on . . . getoutofit!' he turned and slowly loped off towards the gate, stopping to turn and stare at me again. I yelled again, waving my arms, and he jumped the gate and ran off across the lawn. Reluctantly, it seemed.

It was then I took stock of what had happened: in the growing gloom I could see feathers everywhere; no pigeons, just feathers. White ones . . . and grey ones. Still shocked, I called and searched for my three pigeons – and any others (there were always 'hangers-on') that might be lying injured somewhere, including a white ex-patient of mine called Whitey. I couldn't find any of them. I got a torch and searched everywhere, but no trace – just pathetic bunches of feathers here and there. Sadly I came indoors . . .

In the morning Judy and Snowy turned up. It looked as if Punch, Whitey and possibly two grey pigeons had all been killed. Judy and Snowy must have managed to escape by flying on to a roof and it had been too dark the previous evening for me to have seen them – and they would have been too scared to fly down.

That night Judy was alone in her bathroom cage, flying in through the window as usual. Snowy flew into the cage below. I felt awful: it was all my fault that Judy had lost her devoted mate. They'd been more faithful to each other than any pigeons I'd ever known. Now she stood on the perch, waiting for Punch to join her: poor Punch, who couldn't fly at all and hadn't had any chance of escape when the fox struck.

It was three weeks before Judy would allow Snowy to share her bathroom cage. I'd tried them together earlier but she wouldn't have it. Snowy had been busy courting her in the rabbit-hutch during the last two weeks, and, reluctant at first, she'd finally accepted him as her new mate. Four days later, Judy laid her first egg early one morning in the cage. Snowy set about making her a most uncomfortable nest of twigs, very sparse and with a thrown-together-at-the-last-minute look about it; as if Judy had said to him, 'Hurry-up-I've-got-another-egg-to-lay!' Two days later she laid the second egg: pigeons, of course, always lay just two. Then Judy started to incubate.

Meanwhile nine days before the first egg, yet another white

pigeon came to stay – yes, the young girl plumber again! She was even more apologetic; this one had been shot outside some council offices, she said indignantly; she thought they were having a pigeon cull. Like Snowy, this one had a nasty looking wing injury and it was very swollen; she also had a slight head injury, as if the shot had deflected and grazed her head.

The new arrival was put in a smaller cage in the kitchen – the one over the two duck cages – and the injuries cleaned and treated. Four days later the pigeon was well enough to potter around outside and after a while she went up the ramp into the hutch to join Judy and Snowy. The newcomer was eventually called Gonzo. She perched on the half-brick . . .

Judy sat on her two eggs in the bathroom for twenty-seven days, but they failed to hatch. I had assured Eric they wouldn't – he was annoyed that I allowed her to sit on them – though I had no means of knowing whether they would or not. Almost the whole time Judy sat, Snowy stood beside her in the cage. She didn't leave the nest often but when she did 'take a break' and go for a quick fly round outside, Snowy sat on the eggs. Both pigeons ate in the cage during the period of incubation. At the end of the twenty-seven days I thought there was nothing for it but to take the eggs away, so I lifted a reluctant Judy out of the window, Snowy following, and shut the window. I felt sorry for them both. All that time wasted. I'd managed to clean the cage occasionally and stop it smelling – I'd promised Eric I would – but now I gave it a thorough spring-clean and disinfected it well, throwing out the soiled twigs that had constituted a nest.

They spent most of the day outside and that night slept together on the perch in the bathroom cage; back to normal. In the morning they both flew out of the window to spend the day outside in the usual manner. Then it happened: as I returned to the kitchen I heard a noise outside and, looking out, saw Snowy and Judy fly across the lawn with a sparrowhawk on their tail. The three birds, the hawk virtually within inches of them, disappeared from sight over the field and behind some trees.

Horrified – there was nothing I could do – I stood there for several minutes. Would they both be killed? Would one of them manage to escape? They'd been chased right away from the garden now . . .

I kept going outside, hoping against hope to see the two pigeons reappear safe and sound. But it was a good hour before I saw anything further. Then I saw the sparrowhawk bending over something at the side of the small lawn the car-park side of the Chalet: it was the body of poor Judy.

I found Snowy round by the rabbit-hutch. He was unharmed but obviously pretty shocked: he was hiding round the side of the hutch, his head in the corner, shaking. Picking him up I carried him into the bathroom and put him in the cage.

The sparrowhawk had been taking pigeons on and off all the winter. As previously mentioned, there were always 'hangers on'; usually grey feral pigeons that joined any pigeons I had. The hawk also took collared doves occasionally, and sometimes a sparrow or two. He usually pounced on any unwary bird pecking around on the lawn just the other side of the fence, appearing from nowhere and striking as swiftly and silently as the fox. It was all very upsetting: Nature in the raw, I suppose. Foxes and hawks have to eat.

The evening of that same sad day an alarming thing happened to Gonzo in her cage in the kitchen: her 'forehead' – at the top of her beak – lifted off like a lid exposing the inside of her beak and nostrils. She'd had a nasty looking scab form there since she was injured and had been on antibiotics on and off for a long time. Now it looked serious and I hurried to the phone and rang the local vet. He came to see Gonzo and I was advised to keep the open place clean, apply some ointment and hope for the best: he said there was really nothing one could do otherwise and that a kind of skin might well grow over the 'hole' in Gonzo's forehead.

This was how she got her name.

'Reminds me of Gonzo, the Muppet,' remarked Eric one morning as he peered into the cage. 'Hello . . . Gonzo!'

The pigeon certainly had a rather strange appearance and I could see what he meant.

I kept Gonzo indoors and it was about a month before she was allowed outside. The vet was quite right and a skin did eventually form over the U-shaped hole in her upper mandible. But her beak still looked rather peculiar, though it didn't seem to bother the pigeon in the least.

Snowy, who had had an unhappy four weeks himself, immediately started courting her. After Judy's death he'd flatly refused to fly at all for twenty-five days. He was reluctant even to come out of the bathroom and for days I hadn't the heart to move him. When I did persuade him to go outside he went straight into the rabbit-hutch and stayed there all day. Every day. I put corn and water for him in there, knowing how nervous the poor chap was. Not surprisingly.

So Snowy and Gonzo got together and a few days later they mated. Now they shared the same cage in the bathroom at night – the one Snowy had been sleeping in alone. It was then the third week in February.

By May 2nd Gonzo had laid her third clutch of eggs. The previous two clutches she'd completely ignored, though Snowy had dutifully made her a twiggy nest each time in the bathroom cage. She just hadn't wanted to know. Snowy, it was obvious, had wanted her to incubate the first two lots, but Gonzo kept flying off outside and each time left her eggs rolling about on the floor of the cage. If I put them in the nest she'd remove them on her return, pushing them into a corner with her beak and doing this repeatedly, wanting them removed. She wasn't at all keen on being a mum! But Snowy finally talked her into it: the third clutch Gonzo laid she deigned to sit on, fluffing herself out and settling down on the two white eggs in the middle of the new lot of twigs. I'm sure Snowy was glad; he must have been getting fed up with making all these nests. As with Judy, Gonzo arranged the twigs into a rough – very rough – nest when the hard-working Snowy brought them in, but played no part gathering them. Snowy was very fussy about his twigs, picking up and discarding many before taking the selected one in through the bathroom window. I used to watch him and wonder about it.

After seventeen days the eggs hatched: when I uncovered the cage that morning there were two tiny wobbly pink babies with yellow fluff. The proud parents I'm sure were thrilled – so was I! Eric wasn't.

'I can hear baby pigeons in the bathroom,' he announced over a third cup of early morning tea in bed that morning. 'So the eggs *have* hatched? I suppose we're going to have all that mess again.' He stared gloomily into his cup, after glancing at the wall that separated the bedroom from the bathroom.

'As if there aren't enough ruddy pigeons around already,' he added later, grumbling his way into the kitchen.

I explained that the pigeons had had such a rotten time lately, with one thing and another, that I thought they deserved a little happiness – that's why I was pleased about the babies. But I could see my husband wasn't impressed or terribly interested in the happiness of the pigeon population. I sighed, and went back to the bathroom to smile upon the new chicks and their parents.

In six days the eyes of the pigeon chicks began to open. They developed normally, both parents feeding and brooding them and seemingly very proud of their new family: most people thought the chicks 'ugly-looking things' but I liked the two fat, lumpy yellow babies and often popped into the bathroom to admire them; beauty is supposed to be in the eye of the beholder.

When they were old enough I moved the family out into the rabbit-hutch, making a new clean nest of hay (better than Snowy's, I thought) in one corner. Gonzo was a bit put out at first but soon settled down and the feeding and brooding continued, though the growing chicks were gradually left alone for longer periods, one or other of the parents invariably perching nearby.

Four weeks later Snowy caught his ankle in between the top of the ramp and the floor of the hutch. Fortunately I was around to see his distress and free him, but the leg was broken and had to be taped up: I used 'Micropore' for this purpose. After two weeks I was able to remove the tape and the leg had set; Snowy was as good as new again.

Now we had four snowy white pigeons all perching in a row in the hutch. The twins were soon flying and often on the roof with their dad, but Gonzo still couldn't fly.

Eric wasn't too pleased to see four large white pigeons, I'm afraid. But Snowy, Gonzo and I were delighted.

23

Houdini the Long-Tailed Tit

A very different bird was a tiny long-tailed tit fledgling that was found at the side of a country road. He had a broken wing and was lucky to be spotted by a sharp-eyed motorist passing by who stopped, picked up the little bird and brought him to me.

He was a most fascinating little fellow – a real live wire, never still for a minute. He had a pinky/beige and black body no longer than the top joint of my little finger and a very long black-and-white tail. I tried him first in a specially adapted budgie cage with thin twiggy perches and dry soil on the floor and a tuft of grass. His wing didn't seem to bother him at all as he flitted from perch to perch like a tiny animated ball, flicking his long tail, but I doubted if he'd ever fly properly again.

Two things struck me straight away about my tiny patient: one was that he never seemed to rest and the other was his truly amazing appetite. If I had to add a third it would be his ability and desire to escape and go exploring.

The little long-tailed tit's cage was usually out on top of the concrete coal-bunker during the day, partly shaded with a cloth as the weather was very hot and sunny. That first day I covered the cage mid-evening, said goodnight, and half an hour later carried the cage indoors and placed it on my bed. Later, I moved him into Eric's room for the rest of the evening as it was quieter. Almost dark, I went outside some time later to fetch a garden chair indoors, stopping in amazement and staring in disbelief at the sight that met my eyes: there was my tiny long-tailed tit strolling around on the patio. I'd been carefully tending an empty cage!

The following afternoon I put the little bird in his cage in the kitchen while I had a short nap in Eric's room. When I returned the cage was empty! This time I couldn't find the tit anywhere – inside or out – and I was getting really upset and wondering how on earth he'd escaped again when I went to have yet another look outside – and nearly trod on him: he was on the bottom of our three steps up to the front door! Presumably he'd been off exploring again and was just coming home.

I christened him Houdini there and then. I had no idea how he was escaping. I didn't think he could squeeze through the bars of the budgie cage and I certainly wasn't leaving the door open.

'It's no good,' I said to Eric later. 'I'll just have to make him a special cage. He *must* somehow be squeezing through the bars of this one.

Thinking about this, I had an idea: I had some large cardboard lengths that each folded into a square lid. They'd come off some new boxed TV sets and I'd found them near the dustbins some time ago. I was always on the look out for useful-looking cardboard. If I made Twilweld sides these 'lids' would do for the top and bottom of the new cage; not even Houdini could manage to squeeze through half-inch Twilweld – *could* he?

So this I did, stretching out a length of Twilweld on the patio and carefully folding it to form four sides about eighteen inches square. The ends were joined with twists of wire, making sure there wasn't the tiniest gap and that the sides fitted into the cardboard lids perfectly: any mistakes and he'd be out again. It took me all one afternoon. The bottom in place, I then fitted out the new escape-proof cage with perches, soil, water-pot and so on, before fixing the other lid in place as a roof. The cage complete – and looking rather good, I thought – I then cut a five-inch square out of the front and made a little Twilweld door with a paper-clip hook to keep it fastened.

The finished cage was much bigger than the budgie cage and would give the little bird more room to flit about. But I'd forgotten one thing: would it go through the doors into the sitting-room? There was a moment of trepidation as I carried the cage up the steps, but all was well – just! There wasn't an inch to spare.

I put the new cage on the end of the duckling-box on the radiator and put Houdini inside. He wasn't a bit afraid of me and was easy enough to handle and catch. He settled down at once, flitting merrily about, his long tail flicking from side to side as he tried out all the different perches and pottered around on the floor. Soon he was perching near the front of the cage, squeaking for food.

Houdini's appetite had to be seen to be believed; it was insatiable. I'd never known anything like it. All day long he demanded – and got – little bits of food given to him. In the new cage, he always positioned himself on the same perch every time he saw me, eager for more. He ate Go Cat, minced steak, chicken, tongue, earwigs, flies, woodlice and just about anything else in that line offered. He had drinking water in his cage, of course, but I didn't dare leave any food in there; the first time I tried this I put in a small dish full of tasty morsels that were meant to last most of the day; in my naivety I thought it was plenty for so tiny a bird. To my dismay, however, Houdini wolfed down the lot in ten minutes flat. I was convinced he'd burst or be dead within the hour, but, none the worse for this gluttony, he was on the perch jumping up and down, tail swinging, eager and ready for more in no time at all. And so it was, all day and every day. I was in and out all day long feeding him tiny bits of food at frequent intervals. I seldom left him foodless for more than twenty minutes at the very most; usually it was every five or ten minutes – quarter of an hour and the little bird reckoned he was starving to death! But he was so utterly charming and such a gay, happy little chap I didn't mind all this running in and out, though it was somewhat exhausting with so many other birds to feed and tend as well.

One day, while he was in his cage on the coal-bunker as usual, I caught Houdini trying to squeeze through one of the half inch Twilweld squares. He couldn't. But another day when I lifted the cardboard lid top to adjust a perch he gave me the slip, quickly hopping into the undergrowth at the side of the patio, behind the ivy-covered tree stump near the duck-pen, and disappearing.

'Oh, no . . . he's gone!' I wailed. 'Oh *no!*'

'Don't panic,' said the unperturbed Eric, out on the patio sunning himself. He rose slowly to his feet, staring in the direction the tit had vanished. Then, gloomily, 'Hmm. I don't think you'll ever see *him* again.' Words promoting instant panic.

I was bent double, meanwhile, peering into the dense undergrowth and hoping against hope for at least a glimpse of the tiny bird, but it was worse than looking for a needle in a haystack.

'It's no use, it's hopeless . . . he's gone!' I moaned, nearly in tears. 'He'll die if I can't find him . . . he can't fly.'

I was still in the corner where Houdini had disappeared when Eric suddenly said in a stern, quiet voice, 'Come here . . . beside me, slowly! Now look!'

I turned to face him. He'd risen to his feet again and was staring fixedly at a corner of the duck-pen, pointing.

'There!'

Joining him, I followed his gaze and there in the pen near the entrance of the little duck-house was Houdini, unconcernedly pottering around and pecking at the soil, tail swinging gaily. Slowly and stealthily I approached, managing to grab the truant.

'I told you not to panic,' remarked my husband as he sank back into his chair and closed his eyes.

As for little Houdini, safely twittering around back in his cage I could almost imagine him saying, 'What was all the fuss about? I was only having a look round.'

The little long-tailed tit lived with us for six weeks before sadly dying one night. He'd been having a very bad moult and I could only think this was instrumental in causing his death. He'd been slightly off his food for several days and this was so unusual I was worried. Moulting affects some birds more than others and can put a strain on them; perhaps it had been too much for the little fellow? His death was a great shock and I couldn't think of any other possible reason, unless it was something to do with over-eating?

We were both very sad indeed and sorely missed the little bird for a long time afterwards. But I think it is fair to say he'd enjoyed his comparatively short life to the full and it was certainly better than dying at the side of a dusty road.

24

The Kingfisher and the Very Old Magpie

*O*ne day a young couple arrived with a beautiful little kingfisher in a box. They said they'd found him at the side of their garden pond and they thought he couldn't fly.

When they'd gone I examined the little bird but couldn't really find anything wrong: his wings seemed all right and no injury was visible anywhere. I fixed him up in my largest hat-box with a piece of wood to perch on and a deepish water-pot, etc., and then I set about offering him something to eat. First I tried some small slivers of tinned mackerel, but he spat these out, so then I tried sardine: I hadn't any fresh fish. He liked the sardine better and swallowed a few pieces obligingly. I had to forcibly open his incredibly long narrow beak each time and feeding him wasn't easy: the slivers of fish were inclined to fall out the other side instead of going down his throat.

The kingfisher seemed fine next morning and I decided to take him across the fields to the other side of the lake in the woods; the place where I'd released Too-Too, the moorhen who kept returning. It was a perfect place for kingfishers and in the past I'd seen several of these beautiful little birds flit across the water. Arriving at the lake I crouched down about five feet from the edge of the shallow water there, lifting the little bird from the box and holding him in cupped hands. He was struggling, wanting to go, but when I opened my fingers he flopped on the grass in front of me. I picked him up and tried again but the same thing happened; this time he spread his wings, trying to drag himself towards the water.

Sadly, I picked him up again and popped him back in the hat-

119

box, carrying him home. It was 'back to the drawing board'.

The rest of the day I fed the kingfisher more slivers of sardine and this time he took them nicely from a pair of tweezers. I was very pleased he'd learnt to do this as I never really liked having to forcibly feed any bird, though it was sometimes necessary.

The following day the little kingfisher appeared desperate to be off and was very restless, so I thought we'd have another go and so off I trudged once more to the lake. But before this I'd let him fly from my hands across the room and he'd flown perfectly.

Again I crouched down a few feet from the shallow water, holding the bird in my hands, and this time to my delight he flew effortlessly straight across the water to a small island about thirty feet away: a quick flash of brilliant blue and the little kingfisher was out of sight. Marvellous! I felt really elated as I carried the empty box back home.

My oldest patient was a little magpie runt called Jack. Ninette – the girl who brought him – said her mother-in-law had had the magpie, not much larger than a blackbird, for twenty years, ever since he'd been brought to her to rear as a youngster. Now he was a very old man, wet and bedraggled with tatty feathers and a broken ankle. Ninette explained that the magpie had got his foot stuck behind the water-pot in his cage, hence the injury.

I put the little old magpie – I called him Old Jack, to avoid confusion – in the sliding-door cage in the kitchen and made him as comfortable as possible. He had a bed of soft hay, my old tin-lizzie hot-water bottle wrapped in two woolly socks and food and water.

'What does he like best to eat?' I asked Ninette. I'd known her for some time because she used to keep her horse, Charlie, in the field the other side of 'no man's land'.

'Egg,' she replied. 'Mainly egg: that's what he's been having every day.'

'What . . . every day for twenty years?' The mind boggled . . .

'Oh well, he's had other things as well. But egg is his favourite.'

'I see.'

Old Jack was with us for three-and-a-half weeks. I'd taped up his cleanly broken ankle with Micropore and after eleven days I was able to remove the tape and his leg was fine. He had a slight limp but had recovered surprisingly well for such an old bird and he'd been a model patient. During his stay I discovered he also quite liked spaghetti and bread-and-milk, but he wouldn't eat meat of any kind, nor Go Cat.

Sometimes I put Old Jack outside in the garden after the tape came off and when it was a nice day. At first I put him under a heavy wire run I'd acquired, but when he got used to the garden and I was outside to keep an eye on him I let the magpie potter around on the flower-bed and patio. Usually he hid under some large low-down lupin leaves, after a while, as he was a bit scared.

The day came when Ninette and her husband came for little Old Jack and took him home. I'd got really fond of him and was quite sorry to see him go. But the lady who'd had him all those years was happy to see him again. And I'm sure he was pleased to see her too.

Crows, of course, weren't nearly as co-operative as the old magpie had been. None of them. Claud still disliked it outside and had been thoroughly troublesome lately. Sometimes, when forcibly put outside, he made what I called his 'something's-got-me' noise – an agonized long-drawn-out cry that never failed to make me drop everything and rush outside, heart in mouth, expecting to find him being dragged off by a cat or some other predator. But on each occasion he was merely voicing his disapproval of being shut out.

'One day he'll cry wolf once too often!' I said to Eric, after Claud had frightened me yet again. It wasn't like me to make disparaging remarks about any of my birds but Claud really *did* overstep the mark sometimes. In other ways, too. He'd taken to very loud cawing indoors which exasperated both of us at times. He'd do it whenever the television was on or when the phone rang, and often when one was trying to hold a conversation with a visitor. He even started this loud cawing if ever I got out of bed in the night: 'Shut *up*! You'll wake Eric,' I'd hiss, and he'd caw almost non-stop early morning. Consequently I frequently just *had* to bundle him outside and shut the door. You could say the naughty crow was his own worst enemy.

The trouble was nothing whatever stopped Claud cawing when he was in the mood. Definitely a masochist, he just loved being chastised and threatened with all sorts of fates. Slapping him with a folded newspaper or hand only made him caw louder than ever, as did covering the cage.

'Can't you get rid of him?' Eric cried almost daily. I knew how he felt: one felt like strangling Claud on occasions. But I pointed out that he could be 'ever so sweet' in between times.

'He can't . . . he's dreadful . . . *always*!' was the vehement reply.

Life could be very difficult. It could also be full of surprises.

For instance, one day I was in the kitchen preparing lunch when I heard a splashing noise coming from the overflowing zinc bath outside that served as a water-butt under the drainpipe near the window. Thinking it was my little black-headed gull, Gully, indulging in a rare bath – he seldom bathed or went on the pond, unlike other gulls I've had – I looked out of the window and was astonished to see one of the white pigeons floating in the middle of the water like a small boat. He wasn't bathing or splashing about but just quietly floating, wings folded. The 'boat' was Snowy! Two other pigeons were dithering around, one perched on the edge of the zinc bath fluttering a wing and dipping its head in the water, but Snowy floated on serene and unconcerned, obviously enjoying himself. A few minutes later he jumped out, only to return for a quick float two more times. A few days later he repeated the performance and it was to become a habit.

Pigeons seem to like water and I'd often seen two squashed together in a smallish bowlful, just squatting there doing nothing in particular. But I'd never seen one floating like a duck before. I was most amused.

Another surprise concerned a Tufted Duck. She was brought to me as a lost duckling when a day or two old and was reared in the usual manner. I called her Chattanooga, Chatty for short, because these ducks don't quack but make a funny sort of churring, chattering noise instead. She was a dear little thing, dark brown and squat, and very friendly. She flew away one day from the duck-pen. Two months old and fully fledged, she'd grown fidgety and so off she went one sunny morning, presumably heading for the river.

Almost exactly a year later I was standing near our south-facing window in the sitting-room bending over various ducklings in the long box on the radiogram when I heard a strange noise. I had a young Mandarin duck in the left-hand side of the divided box and some mallards in the other side. I lifted each lid in turn, listening, but no, it wasn't any of them making the noise. Puzzled, I straightened up and looked out of the window and there on the edge of the flower-bed, facing me and only four feet away was a little Tufted Duck. She was chattering away like mad and so obviously trying to attract my attention as she looked up at the window. Chattanooga! It *had* to be, because gathered round her were thirteen newly hatched baby ducklings. And I was certain she was asking for help to get her family on to water.

I suppose one could argue that it could have been any tufted duck but I have never before or since seen one in the garden. And who else but my Chatty would stand there looking up at the window and virtually shout away in her own peculiar fashion until she got my attention? She must have been nesting in the thicket or somewhere close by, I thought, and now she knew she had to get her large family to water.

Hurrying outside I lifted the little duck into a box and then set about catching the scattering ducklings. It had been raining and I was bent double, diving in and out of the dripping plants and bushes when my friend, Jill, called to take me shopping. She helped me gather up the frightened and elusive remaining ducklings, and we put Chatty and her family into my newly-made mini-aviary near the rabbit-hutch. They would be safe there until we returned; then I'd decide what to do about them. But when we came back from the town we found four little ducklings still outside the aviary and frantically trying to get to their mum inside, with the rest of the family. The tiny ducklings could run like the wind and although we thought we'd caught them all, these four must have been hiding.

At last all thirteen and the duck were together. Jill had to go home, so early that afternoon my other friend Susan came and we caught the whole family, put them in a box and took them by car to the private lake where I released young mallards. First Chatty and then the thirteen baby ducklings took to the water at once, swimming away across the lake in single file. We heaved a sigh of relief. Not all the babies would survive – they never do – but I hoped at least some of them would . . .

25

Just Another Day

So the months and years went by and birds came and went. Each year I had more than ever brought me: last year it was 268 in all.

My two elderly finches, Chloe the greenfinch and Bully the bullfinch, had both died peacefully in their sleep within six months of each other. I'd had them over eight years and they were adult when brought to me, both injured by cats and unable to fly since. They'd been together all those years and were great friends: various other little birds had joined them at times. I reckoned the little finches must have been the equivalent of eighty or ninety years old in human terms and of course in the wild they'd probably have lived only a fraction of the time.

Their place in the cage had been taken by a little one-eyed sparrow called Suki. I'd had her from a small fledgling and she couldn't fly more than a few feet, her wing as well as her eye having been damaged. She was alone at the moment but loved the mirror she had for company and seemed quite content. On warm sunny days I sometimes put her outside to sun-bathe in the covered duckling run, where she had vigorous dust-baths and water ones – though she would never partake of these indoors, for some reason.

Bill Buster, the blackbird, had a new mistle-thrush, name of Maudie, for company. Rambo was still wolf-whistling louder than ever and still refusing to share his cage with even the most charming of female blackbirds, and Cookie the parakeet – who had started it all – was rather sweet on a pretty little lovebird in a cage next to him: I pushed the cages close together so they could twitter to each other. The ducks, of course, still roamed the lawn. Jack had yet another companion: a brown, rather matronly duck called Mollie. She came from the same farm as Winnie and, as always, he was delighted with her.

Strange friendships amongst the birds always interested me. I had a white dove called Snowdrop who couldn't fly because of a slight wing injury, and he became great friends with another little black-headed gull that had a broken wing, having been hit by a car. The two very different birds became inseparable, spending most of each day standing side by side in the duck-pen beside the pond. There were plenty of pigeons and several other doves around, including Snowy's family, but Snowdrop much preferred the company of his gull and never mixed with them. In the evening the two birds climbed the steps and trotted into the kitchen when I shooed them in for the night. They slept in different cages: Snowdrop in a cage on the cabinet and Gully in the lower duck cage, but sometimes the dove would sneak into the gull's cage before I could stop him and would probably have been happy to remain there all night, if allowed. But Gully's cage was inclined to get rather wet and soggy during the night and I thought it better for Snowdrop to roost on the perch in his own cage. I hope I wasn't being too much of a spoilsport.

And now I must put away my ancient portable typewriter. It is evening and almost time to cover up some of the birds. Claud, awkward as ever, flatly refuses to be covered until the last light has been put out and I'm ready to step into bed: any sooner and he manages to reach through the Twilweld and pull the cover down again. And, of course, caw loudly in protest. Cookie likes to watch television and is the second last to be covered. He is waiting now for his cheese-and-onion crisps and possibly a chocolate-coated peanut or two. Rambo is waiting for his evening bath-water – he has two baths every day – and Eric, nodding off over his crossword, will be hoping to see vague signs of his dinner being prepared.

It has been just another busy day . . .